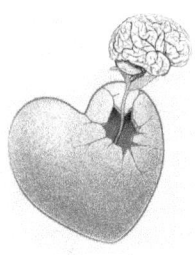

# TESTIMONIALS

"As a licensed clinical professional, I am honored to recommend Blythe as an exceptional Grief and Trauma Recovery expert. She has the unique ability to gently guide an individual's healing process, while simultaneously encouraging healthy decision-making toward lifelong recovery. Partnering with Blythe to create a framework for healthy emotional living will bring years of individual contentment and balance to personal relationships."

– **Tina Guidry**, M.Ed., BCBA, LBA

"As a professional working in the field of trauma for over 40 years, Blythe has written 'the' book about trauma. She is an 'out-of-the-box' thinker who writes meaningfully and with great care. I believe she's on the path to be the next Brene Brown."

– **Kate Ross**

"I've known Blythe Landry for eight years, and her compassion as a trauma, grief, and addiction(s) therapist is beyond measure. She is devoted to helping people find healing in the best, most informed way possible."

– Melinda Morgan

"For anyone who has experienced trauma in their life, this book is a must-read. My early adulthood was full of trauma; I lost my sister at a young age, followed by both of my parents before the age of 40. Blythe has a deep understanding of trauma and how to navigate it. She does wonders for her clients and I'm so excited that she is bringing her deep knowledge to the rest of the world!"

– LaTonya Wilkins, Author of *Leading Below the Surface* and Founder of The Change Coaches, LLC

"For those of us who have had the pleasure of working with Blythe, we all know what a true gift of light she really is—exactly the type of light our world needs right now."

– Jendi Gertz

"Trauma Intelligence Training with Blythe exceeded all my expectations. Her humor, application, and realness were refreshing and made what was, at times, a heavy-hearted topic more approachable and digestible. I learned so much about myself and my relationships. I am better equipped now to support those I love, and also those I teach, from an authentic and educated place. Blythe provided a space for me to be vulnerable and safe, but also to grow. If you are working to understand trauma and its impact, take this training. It is time and money well spent."

– Michelle Tanner Gruntz

"When I first met Blythe in 2015, I was immediately struck by her passion for and immense knowledge of all things related to trauma. As she was a more seasoned and experienced therapist, I frequently leaned on her for knowledge and support with my more difficult cases. As I learned over time, she was a most gracious peer and professional support as we navigated a difficult work situation together. In my several-decades-long career in mental health, I have very seldom come across someone with her integrity, passion, and depth of knowledge. I know that I can count on her to give me excellent and wise counsel as a peer and a professional. I was delighted to hear about her book, as it will enable her to reach many more people."

– **Jeanie Winstrom**, MA LCPC, LPC, LMHC,
Founder, Forever Forward Therapy

"Blythe helped me through the most difficult and painful part of my life. Working with her not only helped me understand all the patterns I act out daily as a result of trauma but also, most importantly, that pain and trauma aren't things that have to control my life. Her help was essential to my recovery journey. For this reason, I recommend her to anyone who needs help like I did. Unfortunately for all of us, she only has so much time in a day and can't take time for the whole planet—that's why I'm thrilled that she is writing this book. So many people could benefit from the knowledge and methods she has developed in her career. I certainly have, and I know others who are hurting will too."

– **T. Meadows**

"Blythe Landry's Trauma Intelligence Training is essential knowledge for every person in today's global society. This highly interactive training provides key principles for understanding the process of how trauma impacts individuals and how to create a safe, supportive environment for someone processing a traumatic experience. Blythe has a unique and easy way of providing clinical knowledge in relatable, understandable lay language that is easily used outside of the classroom. As a trauma survivor, life coach, and yoga teacher, Trauma Intelligence Training has been invaluable in my own trauma recovery and has enabled me to effectively assist my clients in navigating their own experiences in a safe way. I am excited to add her book to my library!"

– **Melissa L. Strawser**, Ed.D., CPC, MBTI

"Blythe brings compassion, thoughtfulness, and a wealth of practical experience to the topic area of Trauma Intelligence. Her Trauma Intelligence course gave me new tools to lead with empathy through the pandemic. It has been so helpful in my corporate role that I recommended it for other colleagues as well. I'm thrilled that she's offering a book on this topic. If you're working through difficulty and determined to find hope, Blythe is a valuable and knowledgeable guide."

– **Melissa Strader**

"Blythe is an inspiration. Her delivery is spot on. Blythe has done an outstanding job of helping me and my team to understand, process, and heal from our own trauma. Her support has created a healthy, positive work environment and has impacted our service delivery to meet our clients' needs in more impactful ways. Ultimately, we all have something to overcome—and this book is a guide in helping us know we're not alone."

– **Jodie Jepson**, Director of Heading Home's ABQ StreetConnect, *Helping the most acute individuals that are experiencing homelessness*

# TRAUMA INTELLIGENCE

# TRAUMA INTELLIGENCE

## The Art of Helping in a World Filled with Pain

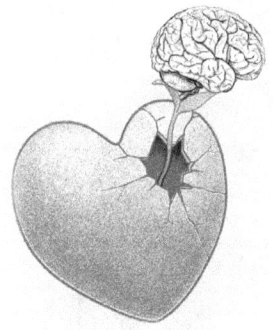

**Blythe Landry, LCSW, M.Ed.**

Copyright © 2021 Blythe Landry, LCSW, M.Ed. All rights reserved.

No part of this publication shall be reproduced, transmitted, or sold in whole or in part in any form without prior written consent of the author, except as provided by the United States of America copyright law. Any unauthorized usage of the text without express written permission of the publisher is a violation of the author's copyright and is illegal and punishable by law. All trademarks and registered trademarks appearing in this guide are the property of their respective owners.

For permission requests, write to the publisher, addressed "Attention: Permissions Coordinator," at the address below.

Publish Your Purpose Press
141 Weston Street, #155
Hartford, CT, 06141

The opinions expressed by the Author are not necessarily those held by Publish Your Purpose Press.

Ordering Information: Quantity sales and special discounts are available on quantity purchases by corporations, associations, and others. For details, contact the publisher at orders@publishyourpurposepress.com.

Edited by: Gina Sartirana
Cover design by: Nelly Murariu
Typeset by: Medlar Publishing Solutions Pvt Ltd., India

Printed in the United States of America.
ISBN: 978-1-951591-91-5 (hardcover)
ISBN: 978-1-951591-90-8 (paperback)
ISBN: 978-1-951591-89-2 (ebook)

Library of Congress Control Number: 2021917778

First edition, October 2021

The information contained within this book is strictly for informational purposes. The material may include information, products, or services by third parties. As such, the Author and Publisher do not assume responsibility or liability for any third-party material or opinions. The publisher is not responsible for websites (or their content) that are not owned by the publisher. Readers are advised to do their own due diligence when it comes to making decisions.

Publish Your Purpose Press works with authors, and aspiring authors, who have a story to tell and a brand to build. Do you have a book idea you would like us to consider publishing? Please visit PublishYourPurposePress.com for more information.

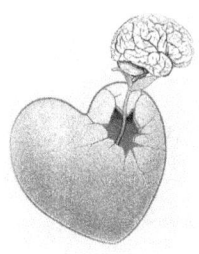

# DEDICATION

This book is dedicated to my sister Marian Henderson and my friend Glendy Mattalia.

Both shining stars. Both gone too soon. And both deserved more time on the planet, making the impact they were intended to make.

Marian Henderson
(1958–2020)

Glendy Mattalia
(1969–2021)

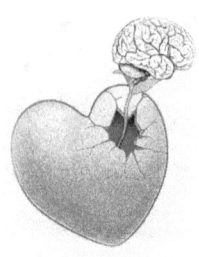

# ACKNOWLEDGMENTS

Jendi Gertz, thanks for being such a great friend and for your vision for this book coming to pass. Thanks also for all of the awesome photographs you have taken of me, including my photo for this book.

Tom Blake, thank you for taking the time to be my first unofficial editor and, of course, for your compassionate, yet raw honesty. Your help, as well as your humor, have been integral in my life and this process.

I would also like to acknowledge my mom, Joyce Landry, as your love of reading and writing, and your support of my writing from my childhood on, have always been an inspiration to me.

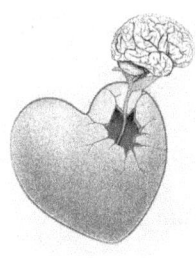

# TABLE OF CONTENTS

| | | |
|---|---|---|
| *Introduction* | | *xv* |
| | Who Are You, and Why Are You Here? | xv |
| | Why Read This Book Now? | xv |
| | What Is Trauma? | xvii |
| | What Is Trauma Intelligence? | xviii |
| CHAPTER 1 | A Break in Consciousness | 1 |
| CHAPTER 2 | Trauma Is Everywhere, But How Do We Identify It? | 5 |
| | 1. Catastrophic Trauma | 6 |
| | 2. Childhood Trauma | 7 |
| | 3. Ambiguous Trauma | 8 |
| | 4. Workplace Trauma | 9 |
| | 5. Communal/Collective Trauma | 10 |
| CHAPTER 3 | Catastrophic Trauma and How It Impacts Our Lives | 13 |
| CHAPTER 4 | Catastrophic Events and Responses: Things to Look Out For | 19 |

| | | |
|---|---|---|
| CHAPTER 5 | Childhood Trauma and How It Impacts Our Lives | 29 |
| CHAPTER 6 | Childhood Trauma: Things to Look Out For | 43 |
| CHAPTER 7 | Ambiguous Trauma and How It Impacts Our Lives | 55 |
| CHAPTER 8 | Ambiguous Trauma: Things to Look Out For | 63 |
| CHAPTER 9 | Workplace Trauma and How It Impacts Our Lives | 71 |
| CHAPTER 10 | Workplace Trauma: Things to Look Out For | 81 |
| CHAPTER 11 | Collective/Communal Trauma and How It Impacts Our Lives | 91 |
| CHAPTER 12 | Collective/Communal Trauma: Things to Look Out For | 97 |
| CHAPTER 13 | Other Types of Trauma to Consider | 107 |
| CHAPTER 14 | Hope for Humanity | 123 |
| CHAPTER 15 | A Second Break in Consciousness | 129 |
| *Bibliography* | | *131* |

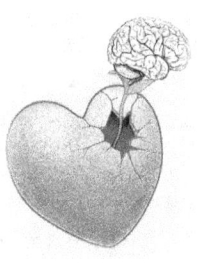

# INTRODUCTION

## WHO ARE YOU, AND WHY ARE YOU HERE?

If you or anyone you have ever known has experienced any type of trauma, and you have opened this book, you are in the right place. Anyone who is willing to learn and implement new ideas related to trauma can become successful in developing Trauma Intelligence. Your education, work status, age, religion, locale, and background are not necessarily indicators of how successful you will be in this process. What are primary indicators of success, however, are your willingness to learn and grow, your desire to understand things that may have once evaded you, and your eagerness to show compassion and empathy in a world that is riddled with pain.

## WHY READ THIS BOOK NOW?

Let's face it. Trauma is everywhere. Even those of us who grew up in seemingly idyllic family environments have, in some place and at some time, experienced an incident that evoked life-altering pain. Add to that the millions of people who have endured abhorrent experiences such as childhood sexual, emotional, mental, physical, and religious abuse. Many of us are walking around acting and reacting to things that we simply have not effectively addressed. These reactions—which are vestiges of past truths and not current realities—serve to diminish our relationships, workplace environments, and communities.

In addition to the potentially negative impact of these reactions on our lives and the lives of those around us, we are also constantly bombarded with catastrophic world events that contribute to and enhance the effects of previously unaddressed, individual trauma.

I suspect that if you are interested in this book, you also believe that we are at a time when it is paramount for us to take mental health more seriously. The way trauma impacts us and those in our lives must be addressed for our families, jobs, and communities. We cannot simply disregard every person and employee who is no longer behaving to our liking, as that would mean disregarding essentially every human being in our lives. Instead of just replacing people, what we need is to find a more reasonable way of recognizing, engaging with, and responding to trauma reactions in ourselves and the people around us.

**Note to the Reader**: When I talk about trauma reactions in this book, I am referring to non-abusive behaviors that limit a person's effectiveness in relationships, families, and workplaces. I am not in any way indicating that sexual, verbal, mental, financial, or physical abuse should ever be tolerated in these settings, nor am I advocating for staying connected to people who are exhibiting this level of abuse. When I discuss trauma reactions, I will be referring to and giving examples of behaviors that diminish connection and productivity, and that are workable and amenable to change and growth. This disclaimer is very important. If you are in an abusive relationship or situation at this time, this book is not intended to allow you to excuse unacceptable behavior. It is intended to help you differentiate between what is allowable and what is not, and learn how to respond more compassionately to the allowable reactions to people's wounds.

## WHAT IS TRAUMA?

In the most basic sense, trauma is the reaction to pain. More expansively, it is the experience of something deeply troubling or disturbing that yields a strong impact on the person experiencing it. Trauma can be sexual, emotional, mental, intellectual, physical, and religious, to name some of the most prominent categories. It can be caused through ill intention from the person perpetrating it, or through an unexpected and accidental series of events over which the person experiencing it has no control.

To many people, traumatic experiences are obvious: witnessing an accident or being in one, being present during a mass shooting, or having a loved one impacted by such an event. But trauma can also be—and in many cases is—far more complex and nuanced.

Repeated abuses by caregivers or within personal relationships damage the receiver in confusing and lasting ways. More definitively, most traumas are not the result of things like plane crashes or the murder of a friend (although those are certainly traumatic events). The majority of trauma comes through long-term exposure to abuses we either could not escape (in the case of children), or where we felt totally disempowered to escape due to previous traumatic experiences coloring our perspective. Feeling trapped or terrified are normal reactions to traumatic experiences.

## WHAT IS TRAUMA INTELLIGENCE?

Trauma Intelligence includes, but is not limited to, a commitment to learning about and improving one's understanding of trauma and how it impacts us as individuals, families, colleagues, and community members. It is the willingness to look within, to notice one's own blind spots to empathy and compassion, and to be open to responding in more effective and understanding ways.

A person who works toward Trauma Intelligence is able to engage with others who may be operating from a place of pain, and to provide a safe environment for continued growth and success. Trauma Intelligence focuses on an empowerment perspective, rather than one of diminished relational and workplace returns.

In addition to helping people become more intentional in responding to others who are coping with trauma, Trauma Intelligence is also about finding more compassion for oneself and one's own recurring or repetitive responses coming from past pain rather than current reality.

When striving toward Trauma Intelligence, we choose to seek more common ground with the people around us and thus, attempt to create a better life experience for both ourselves and those in our lives who matter to us the most.

Trauma Intelligence is not about making excuses for inexcusable behavior; rather, it is about making accommodations for minimizing the pain and suffering in the world.

# CHAPTER 1
# A BREAK IN CONSCIOUSNESS

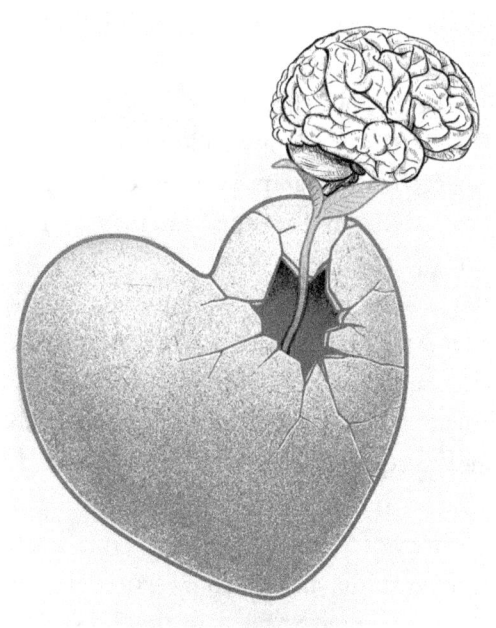

In the summer of 2020, I received a startling call from my sister Sonny in New Orleans. She reported that our eldest sister, Marian, had unexpectedly had a seizure and heart attack at the same time and most likely would not survive. To say I was shocked at that moment would be an understatement. I knew that I wanted to help, but given the situation, I was utterly powerless to do so.

My first thought was of the fear of losing someone I loved unexpectedly and what that might mean for my life going forward. My second thoughts included:

> How much pain was my sister in before this happened? How much of the life that she had lived up to that point had been a positive experience for her, and how much of it had been affected by her past traumas and pain? What might her life be like if she did, in fact, survive, or if she could work through that trauma and heal on a deeper level?

A most integral point had come for Marian. A moment of reckoning. A moment of two possible roads, over which she had no control, emerged: one that meant she would get another chance at this thing called life, and another that meant the end of her life was imminent.

Twelve days after my sister lost consciousness, she passed away. The heart attack and seizure had left her hypoxic for around twenty minutes, and her brain simply could not recover. Unlike those of you who are alive and reading this book, she did not get another chance to turn her life and her story around. She had just turned 62.

While the story of Marian's departure from Earth is undoubtedly relevant to my life, my personal experience with this loss isn't what I hope to impart to you in this book. What I suggest you draw from this is the reminder of the finite nature of life;

## A BREAK IN CONSCIOUSNESS

I spoke to my sister on a Monday, and by Tuesday, she was no longer conscious. There is a limited amount of time we all have in which to face ourselves, face our traumas, and transform our hurts. But you do not have to wait until there is an 'end,' in your own life or for those who you love, for you to begin a process of intentional change—of willingness to face your own demons. You do not need to wait until a crisis comes before your existence on this planet becomes one of immeasurable peace and, more importantly, immeasurable purpose.

It is my wish for you in reading this book that you gain both a more compassionate lens toward yourself, and a more productive and empathic approach to relating with the people in your life whom you encounter every day.

CHAPTER 2

# TRAUMA IS EVERYWHERE, BUT HOW DO WE IDENTIFY IT?

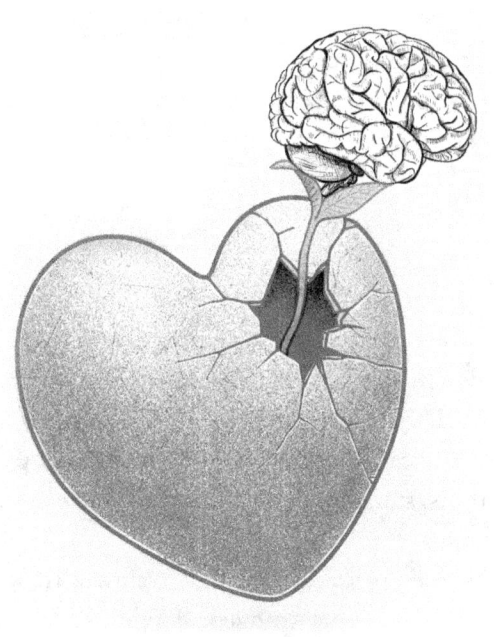

If you have already picked up this book, I don't need to tell you that the traumas we carry from the past into the present have a lasting and profound impact on our daily lives. I also don't have to tell you that not only do our unresolved traumas impact the people with whom we regularly interact, but that the traumas of those we care about are equally impacting us. We cannot change what has happened in the past, to ourselves or to those we love, but we absolutely can change how we respond moving forward.

When it comes to trauma, we often confuse the distinction between cause and response. Many of us walk around thinking that the things that happened to us were not 'bad enough' to associate with the word trauma, because maybe our pain doesn't seem as tragic as someone else's pain. So, in order to dispel the myth that an event must be the worst thing that ever occurred in anyone's life to constitute trauma, let's distinguish between types of traumas and the potential impact those have on the average person.

Large concepts are always more digestible in smaller chunks—so for our purposes, let's break trauma down into five major categories.

## 1. CATASTROPHIC TRAUMA

Examples of this type of trauma include, but are not limited to: loss through a natural disaster, a serious accident that may or may not include death, kidnapping, the murder of a loved one, an incident of physical/sexual assault in adulthood, witnessing a violent act or event, or witnessing the harming of another person. Shootings, natural disasters, and car crashes could also fall under this type of trauma.

When it comes to catastrophic trauma, there are several important factors to take into consideration. While the word 'catastrophic' may make this sound more painful than the other types of trauma, that is not necessarily the case. In this context, I encourage you to think of catastrophic trauma as related to a sudden event that causes a painful and long-lasting reaction in the people who experience it.

In addition, how a particular event affects anyone who knows about it is relevant when considering catastrophic trauma. For example, repeatedly seeing or hearing the details of a tragic event via the media can also increase the number of people deeply impacted by it. Research has found that television media coverage of both natural and man-made disasters is associated with negative mental-health impacts including depression, anxiety, and posttraumatic stress disorder.[1]

Our response to catastrophic trauma, as well as our ability to heal from it, is directly related to our experiences in childhood. If we have a substantial amount of childhood trauma, our responses to calamitous trauma can include both a reaction to the specific tragic event as well as responses rooted in wounds from the past that resurface as a result of the catastrophe. This can also be true for other types of trauma that may have occurred prior to this event and/or simultaneously.

## 2. CHILDHOOD TRAUMA

Childhood trauma can include sexual abuse/molestation/incest, physical abuse, intellectual abuse, mental abuse, religious abuse, emotional abuse, or neglect. Generally speaking, where there is one type of trauma in childhood, there are others.

---

[1] Betty Pfefferbaum et al., "Disaster Media Coverage and Psychological Outcomes: Descriptive Findings in the Extant Research," *Current Psychiatry Reports* 16, no. 9 (September 27, 2014): p. 464, https://doi.org/10.1007/s11920-014-0464-x.

Childhood trauma is in its own category for two reasons. First, children are often dependent on their abusers for food, attention, clothing, shelter, and care. This dependence means the abused child must remain, without any options, in a terrifying and unsafe circumstance in order to survive. Second, children are reliant on their caregivers and role models to teach them things like safety, connection, relational expression, and love. When those messages are interspersed with abuse, a child's brain develops amid confusing signals and heightened central nervous system responses that follow them throughout their development. Until childhood trauma is addressed through professional help, it will continue to follow people throughout their adult lives.

## 3. AMBIGUOUS TRAUMA

Ambiguous trauma can sometimes fall under childhood trauma. However, it can occur at any stage or age in one's life. Ambiguous trauma is generally a recurring loss—one that does not necessarily have an identifiable origin, but continues to cause grief, heartache, and even devastation over a long period of time. An example of ambiguous trauma is growing up or living with an active alcoholic and watching a parent, partner, child, or other loved one change over time due to the addiction.

Ambiguous trauma can also occur when you love someone who has a traumatic brain injury; is diagnosed with Alzheimer's disease; has suffered a stroke or an accident; or has changed mentally, intellectually, or physically. It also includes feelings of loss around a familiar pattern of living that changes your circumstances over time. In a situation where a person changes due to illness, that individual's caregiver can be traumatized. Amid an uncertain future, there may be deep hurt about this new reality and how it differs from the person's original plans for the future.

Ambiguous trauma can also come from living under the constant threat of losing your job or home, or from an abusive living situation where you feel unsafe or disempowered to escape. Ambiguous trauma is something that you see or know about on a daily basis, but can't necessarily get away from; the grief is ongoing, with no end in sight.

## 4. WORKPLACE TRAUMA

Most of us spend the majority of our lives working, so it makes sense that we can experience trauma related to our jobs. Police officers, emergency medical technicians (EMTs), firefighters, doctors, nurses, and others working in immediate response to either crime and/or medical emergencies are at particular risk for workplace trauma due to the nature of their jobs. Workplace trauma can also come from working in potentially dangerous situations—for example, one where large machinery creates a danger of physical harm and/or death.

One well-known form of workplace trauma— and one beyond the scope of what we address in this book—is the trauma of a veteran returning to civilian life from combat. This type of trauma is a very serious and substantial form of post traumatic stress disorder (PTSD) that leaves veterans in a world where things that once made sense no longer do. Veteran trauma leaves the person fearful of and reactive to horrifying circumstances, even in the absence of the possibility that those circumstances would happen in 'typical' or civilian life.

Another less-obvious and less-discussed, but common, form of trauma on the job is an abusive or toxic work environment. This can include long-term racism, sexism, ageism, and/or ableism (to name a few) a person may be subjected to over a period of time in their place of employment. Feeling stuck in any unhealthy situation, where either employees are allowed to abuse one another or managers are allowed to abuse staff, can be harmful and even life altering. These types of workplace traumas consistently diminish your feelings of safety and security when experienced over a long period of time. When the toxic circumstances are pervasive, the resulting workplace trauma can lead to effects like decreased self-esteem, increased anxiety, increased mental health challenges, and even financial anxiety and loss.

## 5. COMMUNAL/COLLECTIVE TRAUMA

Communal and/or collective trauma involves some group of people who experience a similar, life-altering event or series of events at the same time. The COVID-19 pandemic is a perfect example of collective trauma. Another example would be a global war, a catastrophic bombing, or widely felt event like the terrorist attacks of September 11, 2001.

Other types of collective trauma may include, but are not limited to: an entire community being ravished or decimated due to a natural disaster or crime spree; or the loss of a large group of loved ones, such as an entire family, many members of a sports team, or the death of a beloved public figure, in a specific community.

The main distinguishing factor of collective trauma from other traumas is that, generally speaking, it can potentially make people feel closer to their peers and less alone in their coping process—even as they still are in a lot of pain. In contrast, the other four types of traumas tend to make us feel isolated, ashamed, and completely confused about our realities.

As you look at the list of collective/communal traumas, you may notice that some of them could also be considered catastrophic traumas. Some traumas fall into more than one category, but the important distinguishing factor in collective/communal trauma is that the loss or trauma impacts a large group of people all at once. Those affected people can then relate to one another based on their shared traumatic experience. As we move forward in the book, this distinction will be important to remember.

## CALL TO ACTION

Now that I've laid out the five main categories of trauma, it is time to take some action. Let's start with you. We can always work to understand others better by first taking stock of ourselves. Please take out either a piece of paper or a journal and a pen (writing, not typing, is preferable) and make a list of any and all of the relevant categories in which you have felt traumatized.

Once you have completed that task, circle any items on the list that surprised you. Then put a star next to the ones that you hadn't realized, until now, would constitute as traumas.

It will be important for you to have this list with you as you continue with the rest of this book.

If you start to write things down and you feel any sense of panic, anxiety, or angst that feels unsafe or insurmountable to you, please pause, close the book, and do not reopen it until when and if you feel safe to move forward. If you feel extremely triggered, please contact your closest friend or mental health professional. This book is intended to be educational, not a trauma recovery plan, and it should not be a replacement for proper and seasoned professional help.

CHAPTER 3

# CATASTROPHIC TRAUMA AND HOW IT IMPACTS OUR LIVES

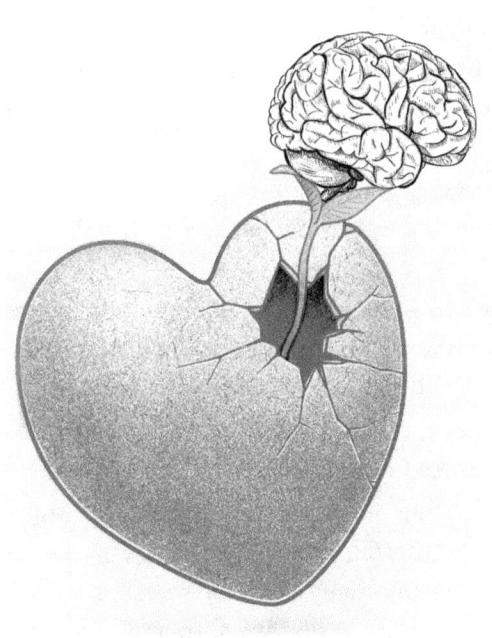

Imagine that you're walking around at a concert, having a good time, singing along to the music and holding hands with your significant other. Then, out of nowhere, the person next to you gets shot and badly hurt, or even killed. As a result, your central nervous system will experience an abrupt and sudden shift in ways that are almost indescribable. Just a few moments earlier, you loved crowds and parties and holding hands with your significant other; but after witnessing such a catastrophic event during a defenseless and vulnerable moment, every single one of those things could become a trigger for you going forward.

Maybe when you hear that music—or any type of music—again, you feel your heart racing or see images of something dark and gruesome that you cannot get out of your brain. Maybe when you see a crowd on television, your entire system begins to shut down—you forget what day it is or where you are. Maybe when your significant other tries to hold your hand, your palms start to sweat and you feel like you might pass out.

Does all this mean you don't like music or television or that you don't love your partner? No. It means that an event that happened when you couldn't have predicted it and least expected it jolted your body, your brain, and your entire consciousness in a way that has essentially stolen the joy in those luxuries from your being.

And does this mean you can never in your entire life find any joy in any of those things again? Absolutely not. But it does mean that doing so will require a new way of learning, engaging, and being that, prior to this event, you never had to be bombarded with or had a need to rationalize.

The first thing we usually associate with trauma is a catastrophic or life-altering event like a shooting. One of the things I have found in my many years of working with clients, families, and communities is that we absolutely do not all experience this level of trauma equitably. Some of us walk through life never losing a loved one in an accident or to murder, never having an earth-shattering car crash, never losing our physical mobility, and never being in a music venue when a mass shooting occurs. Others of us walk around having experienced one, two, or even five (or more) of these events. To go too deep into why this may or may not be would be to delve into areas of spirituality not within the scope of this book; however, that differentiation is definitely worth noting. What we need to remember, most crucially in relation to catastrophic-event trauma, is this: **The person we were before the event can be, in some cases, almost unrecognizable to the person we are after the event.**

Think back to the imaginary scenario that opened this chapter. Now, let's say your significant other was on the other side of you when the shooting occurred. They heard the shot fired at the person next to you—but were so engaged in the music and holding your hand, or perhaps talking to someone on the other side of them, that they didn't see the actual event that you saw. Maybe they didn't even realize it was a gunshot until they heard you screaming. Your significant other may have experienced a different type of trauma, a trauma of confusion in a moment where they didn't comprehend the reality of what was happening. Maybe they experienced the trauma of seeing you frightened and not understanding why. They may even have suffered a trauma of dissociation that left them totally unaware of what was going on around them.

What then might happen to your relationship? What might occur when they don't understand anymore why your standing next to them now makes you terrified and scared? What if their response to that trauma is to want to cling to you even more, emotionally and physically? What if your response, in return, is to want to run as far away as possible because any time you even look down at their hand, your breathing becomes difficult and your heart starts to race?

In this situation, one of two things is going to happen. Either one or both of you are going to get some serious professional help for your trauma reactions and learn to respond to one another in ways that are safe and make sense, or you are going to completely lose sight of what you had before this event and, sadly, then lose sight of one another as well.

This is an example of a ripple effect of trauma, a secondary effect, if you will. Basically, one trauma can lead to another trauma of relational confusion and loss, resulting in further isolation, discomfort, and even shame. The precipitating catastrophic event is just the beginning of the myriad ways this trauma will domino and impact your lives.

In this example, your significant other and you would have gone through a trauma of the same event but processed it in such a different way that, ultimately, you could lose your connection and your relationship as a result.

■ ■ ■

Let's look at another type of catastrophic trauma: a car accident that leaves a father, who was driving, alive but his son dead. The father was not drunk or texting or doing anything that may have been the cause of a 'fault-related' accident. He was simply driving and swerved to avoid hitting a deer in the road, which then led him to lose control of the vehicle and crash into a tree. When the impact occurred, the father was not knocked unconscious, so he could see that his son had been ejected out of the car—but he was powerless to help. He was trapped in the driver's seat and had to be removed from the car by the first medical responders on the scene.

Later, when the father was in the hospital being treated for serious injuries, a police officer arrived to inform him that his son had, in fact, passed away at the scene. The father is now not only in physical and emotional duress from a horrifying event, he also has to process, from a trapped place in a hospital bed, that due to an accident while he was at the wheel, his own son is dead.

While this situation may seem like too much for any one person to bear, this is really only the beginning of the father's trauma related to this catastrophic and accidental event.

Once the father is out of the hospital, he has to go home—to a home where his wife, with whom he was already having marital difficulties, blames him for the death of their son. She knows intellectually the accident was not intentional in any way, but she is distraught and looking for someone or something to blame. Additionally, the couple's other child, a daughter, shuts down so completely after the loss of her brother and the dissension between her parents that she begins to withdraw and go into a serious depression. She stops engaging in daily activities and starts failing at school. Because both parents are at the literal bottom of life at this point, they have zero energy or tools for helping their daughter, and, thus, she will most likely continue to spiral into a place of negative and painful reactions to the catastrophic event that has essentially destroyed an entire family.

In addition to the immediate family's devastation from the death of this child, the extended family and friends are suffering as well. Grandparents are unable to pull themselves out of the depths of their despair. One grandparent who had been sober for twenty years begins to drink again. The boy's best friend becomes nonfunctional at school and starts being aggressive with his peers, and the best friend's parents also pull away from the boy's parents. While the parents need support now more than ever; the pain of the loss, as well as the effects it has had on their living son, makes it too hard for them to show up and cope.

What started as a driver swerving to avoid harming a deer became an event that forever changed the course of numerous people's lives and will reverberate for many years to come.

■ ■ ■

This is a really integral thing to understand about catastrophic trauma: Even though it is seemingly a one-time event, that event informs our perceptions of life and reality in such an impactful way that everything and every relationship around us is subject to unrecognizable change and, potentially, more loss.

Loss begets loss begets more and more loss.

This type of trauma leads to a chain reaction of pain that can seem invisible, yet impacts every single area of the lives of those who experienced it.

---

### CALL TO ACTION

Take out that list you made in Chapter 2. Put a recognizable symbol next to every event you have experienced that you would classify as a catastrophic/life-altering event trauma on that list. (If there are none that you relate to in that way, that is okay too.) Do not pressure yourself to fit yourself into categories in which you do not; however, if there is a relevant example, make sure to add it. Keep that list with you as you go into the 'Things to Look Out For' section in the next chapter.

---

# CHAPTER 4

# CATASTROPHIC EVENTS AND RESPONSES: THINGS TO LOOK OUT FOR

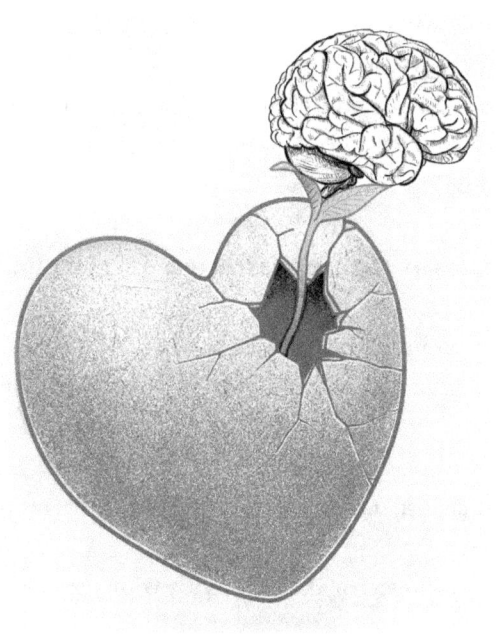

In the last chapter, I outlined some of the significant changes that can happen to a person after experiencing a catastrophic-event trauma. Now let's dig a little deeper, into daily behaviors you may want to pay attention to if you care about someone who may have endured this type of experience. Under each behavioral reaction to catastrophic trauma, I will also provide a brief description of suggested responses and support mechanisms to offer.

## TYPICAL WAYS CATASTROPHIC TRAUMA SHOWS UP IN DAILY LIFE

### *Extreme Startle Response*

If you live with or work with someone who has experienced a catastrophic trauma, you may have recognized they are very quick to startle. One common extreme startle response is that a person you live with can know you are home but still jump and scream when you walk into a room where they are alone. This reaction does not mean they are afraid of you; but it can mean that they have a compromised central nervous system that was directly impacted by their trauma.

**Some examples of extreme startle responses include:**

- Jumping up in terror.
- Screaming/yelling as though they don't know who you are.
- Shaking.
- Hiding and/or ducking.
- Unusual lashing out or anger when they feel trapped or unable to escape.
- Seeming annoyed or irritated with your presence.

# CATASTROPHIC EVENTS AND RESPONSES: THINGS TO LOOK OUT FOR

These responses can be very confusing if you are the person living or working with someone who reacts that way, especially if you have not had the same experience or reaction to an event. Expecting that this reaction could occur and accommodating it accordingly can minimize the challenges experienced for the person affected. Think of it as similar to how you would of course accommodate a friend or colleague who had a physical disability.

**Some recommendations for accommodation include:**

- Text the person to let them know you would like to talk to them before you enter the room that they are in.
- Come up with a safe word with the person prior to entering their space, so that they can begin to associate that word with someone approaching them.
- If possible, let them know when you will be gone and when you expect to return, so they know to expect you when they hear you coming in.
- Work on a system where outside of emergencies, you usually let that person approach you first. This is especially valuable when you and the affected person live together.

These accommodations may seem time-consuming; however, they can help minimize confusion and hurt on both people's parts—and also show the affected person that you care enough to make an effort. Responses and accommodations can't and won't be perfect, but this noticeable effort from a loved one creates a marked increase in the sense of safety the survivor feels in their environment. If you're the person experiencing the trauma responses I've described, you can ask the people you love to help you through these accommodations.

An extreme startle response can be present with each type of trauma we cover in this book. However, it is important to explain why individuals who have experienced a catastrophically traumatic event tend to fall into periods of depression, shut-down, and withdrawal.

## *Depression/Withdrawal*

As mentioned previously, the shock to the central nervous system after experiencing an unexpected and damaging event is palpable and potentially permanently altering. Life may have once seemed free, open, and effortless to the impacted person, but the post-traumatic stress disorder that can follow a life-altering event can lead to feelings of despair and confusion. As well, bizarre behavioral manifestations of catastrophic trauma may make the survivor feel ashamed and lead them to pull away from the people in their life for fear of being judged or criticized.

Catastrophic trauma also changes a person's fundamental perception of their world. Someone who once saw the world as a safe place may no longer view it that way. The person may begin to see everyday places like the grocery store as dangerous, a place where anything could happen at any time. They may begin to assume that others don't have their best intentions in mind, or that they cannot predict when or where something tragic could happen. This shift of perception can alter one's beliefs about everything from the decency of humanity to deep and profound questions about spirituality and the purpose of life.

When your outlook on life goes from 'safe and secure' to 'guarded and afraid,' it is only natural to go through periods of extreme depression and withdrawal. Add to all of that what we learned in the last chapter that loss begets loss begets more relational loss—and the very fabric of the trauma survivor's life has most likely dramatically altered. That can also compound periods of darkness and isolation.

**Some examples of how depression and withdrawal show up in the survivor:**

- Showing less enjoyment in things they may have previously seen as fun.
- Showing less interest in connecting with family, friends, and community members.
- Having a heightened period of withdrawal during the anniversary period of the event.
- Eating more or less than usual.
- Sleeping more or less than usual.
- Forgetting important dates, times, and details about conversations, when once they were really good at that sort of thing.
- Finding ways to be alone, even if they live with other people.
- Pulling away in an obvious way from their most significant relationships.

If you love someone with post traumatic stress disorder (PTSD) due to a catastrophic event, it can be very confusing and painful to be close to them while they are experiencing this. For this reason, practicing self-care and accommodations for both yourself and the affected person are integral.

**Some recommended accommodations for the survivor include:**

- Give them space in ways that feel intentional and productive—not by ignoring, punishing, or lashing out because they are having a hard time.
- Communicate clearly that you recognize a change in them and want to let them know you care enough to notice.
- Tell them that if they do want to talk, you are there to listen.
- Let them know that if they don't want to talk, you will give them space.

- Remind them of important things they may be forgetting.
- Encourage engagement in life, without pressuring them to just "be positive" or just "be grateful."

**Some recommended accommodations for you as the loved one of a survivor:**

- Majorly increase self-work and care including exercise, healthy eating, connecting with other friends who are currently more available.
- Remind yourself of who this person is when they aren't going through a low period, and use *that* as a litmus test for the health of the connection, not this temporary dark period.
- Find ways to be creative and engaged in inspiring activities that don't have to include the other person.
- Talk to shared contacts about how you can all work together to support the person you care for during this time of crisis.

It is important to note that these periods of withdrawal should not last indefinitely. If they do, it is crucial to have a candid conversation with the survivor about the level of care they are seeking and your hope that they will continue to get the mental health support necessary for their recovery. And as stated at the beginning of the book, a person's trauma is never an excuse for them to abuse you or to totally disregard your equally important needs.

This time of offering accommodations is about discovering how you can support the other person while also equally looking out for and supporting yourself and your own needs. You should not remain indefinitely in any relationship (partnership or friendship) where your own needs can never be addressed. To do so would mean that you are undoing yourself to make room for the other person's trauma. Trauma Intelligence is about compassion and effective engagement, not self-abandonment and personal rejection.

## *Periodic Outbursts of Anger/Frustration*

When someone experiences a catastrophic event, it is normal to feel a tremendous amount of fear both during it and afterward. Add on what we have discussed around lost relationships and diminished feelings of safety/trust, and that fear can turn into more deeply entrenched emotions like anger and frustration.

When we carry around that anger and frustration for extended periods of time, it can lead to both internalized rage and outrage at the people we love and trust the most.

**Some examples of how anger and frustration may show up in a person after a catastrophic event:**

- Controlling behavior: wanting the house to be immaculate at all times; trying to control plans in a very obvious way, when that was previously not typical behavior; wanting to do all work projects solo rather than collaborate in groups.
- Exhibiting a shorter fuse or lack of frustration tolerance: impatience with very small mistakes in others; raising one's voice in meetings, when this was once not typical behavior; bursting out of a room for no obvious reason; slamming doors.
- Pushing people away emotionally due to a fear of more loss, through insults, impatience, and/or a lack of availability.
- Picking fights when things seem calm and positive.
- Becoming more aggressive/guarded in public: someone accidentally bumps into them at the store and they react as though it was intentional; impatient with customer service professionals; more verbal and angry toward other drivers.
- Physical violence, though this is rare.

**Some recommended accommodations include:**

- If the person becomes more aggressive or impatient with you, calmly remind them you care about and are there for them, but that it hurts you when they take things out on you.
- During periods of increased volatility, take a step back and allow the person space to connect to their own pain, rather than allowing them to use you as a vessel for acting out that pain.
- Offer workplace accommodations/support in the way of Employee Assistance Program (EAP) counseling, supportive communications, trainings, and safe discussions around appropriate behavior in the workplace.
- Encourage positive outlets for anger expression, such as long, vigorous walks together; screaming together in a safe space; offering to listen to them when they need to vent; and encouraging them to write things down and share them with you or another safe person.
- Avoid fighting back, screaming louder, or attacking as this will only exacerbate the anger and reaction in the other person.

We are often taught that anger makes us bad—but when it comes to processing trauma and grief, anger is absolutely normal and necessary. Responses to a person expressing rage in healthy ways should include loving boundary setting with an acknowledgement that the underlying pain is both valid and safe to talk about. Sometimes when people are feeling afraid and angry, they need a safe person nearby to remind them that they have other options for expressing their anger.

It is also important to remember that abusive rage, and/or physical violence should not be accepted by anyone, no matter how much we love or care for the person exhibiting those behaviors.

# CATASTROPHIC EVENTS AND RESPONSES: THINGS TO LOOK OUT FOR

This is about Trauma Intelligence—that means accommodating and supporting, not avoiding red flags and destructive tendencies.

One good litmus test for whether you will continue to be patient with another person's rage outbursts is whether or not they are acknowledging them as a problem. Another is if they are willing to get the appropriate level of professional help to cope with these reactions to their trauma. If both of those things are present, that is a good sign the person is not only willing to move past their pain-based reactions, but that they most likely will.

There are many other ways that a person will react to and exhibit trauma around a catastrophic event in their daily lives. The three suggested above are a great place to start in deepening your understanding and empathy toward those who are struggling, as well as in enhancing your own Trauma Intelligence in your responses.

## CALL TO ACTION

Take out that list you made in Chapter 2 and remind yourself of any events you identified as catastrophic/life-altering. Which, if any, of the behaviors discussed in this chapter have you noticed in either yourself or others as a result of experiencing one or more calamitous events?

Reflecting on those behaviors, spend some time journaling about how you have responded, to both yourself and others, and how you may want to practice new/more effective responses going forward. If you are the person who has experienced the event(s), how might communicating some of what you learned above to your family and loved ones help you feel more supported? If you love someone who has experienced such an event or events, how might tweaking your responses enhance your connections and your feelings of being supportive?

Spend some time reviewing everything you noted in your list and your answers so far. If new memories pop up for you throughout your learning, go back and add them to your list or edit existing entries as needed. Even though you started your list with a focus on your own personal traumas in our first "Call to Action" section; it is okay to begin to add in events that have impacted the people in your life as well.

CHAPTER 5

# CHILDHOOD TRAUMA AND HOW IT IMPACTS OUR LIVES

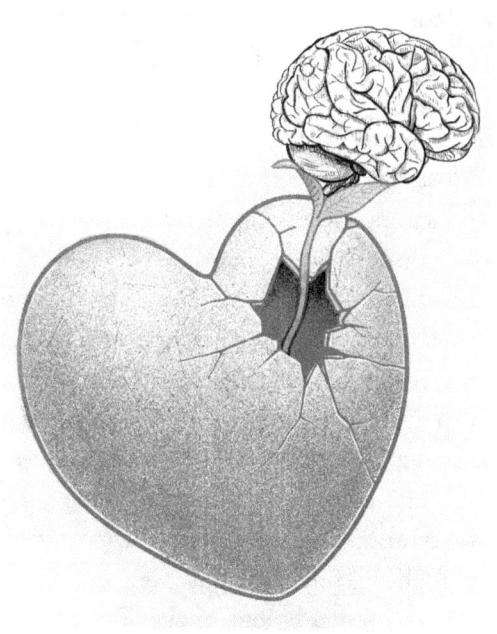

**Note:** It is really important to begin by saying that if you have a substantial amount of childhood trauma, this chapter could be very triggering for you. Please do not force yourself to read anything that makes you too uncomfortable, and remember that you can put this book down at any time if you need a break, and/or simply skip to the next chapter.

Childhood trauma is unique from other traumas due to the important nature of that developmental time in our lives. Trauma that is rooted in childhood often means that as children, when we were supposed to feel safe and secure, someone we depended on violated our trust. When this happens to us as little ones, we cannot fully process or understand the impact until we are older. When we are young we rely on our caregivers to support us in ways that make sense and are reliable. When the people we look to for love and nurturing turn into child abusers, we are subjected to experiences that literally take away the foundation of feeling safe in the world around us.

When an adult who had a functional childhood, without any abuse or neglect, experiences a catastrophic trauma, this person's response will be rooted in an already established framework of safety in the world. However, a person with childhood trauma who later experiences a catastrophic trauma—or any other type separate from their childhood trauma—will not only react to the life-altering event in adulthood, but also to the underlying framework of fear and anxiety in their orientation to the world. This difference is integral to understanding their trauma response, because it reflects the perspective from which a person with childhood trauma lives, as opposed to that of someone who grew up with a sense of security and trust in the people they looked up to most.

Childhood trauma takes many forms. There are the most obvious ones: sexual abuse, physical abuse, emotional abuse, neglect, mental abuse, and even religious abuse. These are recognizable chasms in a child's emotional development that continue to show up in their relationships, workplaces, and communities well into adulthood.

There are also more nuanced types of childhood trauma that can be more difficult to define. One example of this type of trauma is growing up with an emotionally erratic parent who exhibits extreme and confusing mood swings. Living with a parental figure who is emotionally unstable and totally unpredictable yields severe relational trauma in survivors. The adult children of emotionally inconsistent parents (often the result of the parent's own past, unresolved traumas) can be plagued by questions like:

- Who is safe and unsafe?
- How do I become perfect in order to avoid being in trouble some of the time, and getting praise other times?
- Why do I find myself drawn to people who are mean and running from people who truly care?
- Why am I so hard on myself or so afraid of someone leaving me?

Other traumas, such as witnessing the abuse of a sibling or parent, can be equally debilitating. This type of painful and confusing event makes the child feel helpless to aid the person they love who is being harmed. It may also leave the child feeling responsible for their parent, leading to behaviors like jumping in the middle of an argument, even when it means putting themselves in danger.

■ ■ ■

The first example of how childhood trauma impacts a child well into adulthood focuses on a syndrome often referred to as the Parentified Child. I use this example because it can be a more subtle form of childhood trauma, albeit one that shows up all too often and is under-discussed and understood. Learning about this syndrome will give you a glimpse into how childhood trauma is generational—and how even well-meaning parents can transfer trauma to their children because of their own wounds.

As children, we really should only have one job: to be children. Unfortunately, in some families, there are dynamics that lead to children being treated like para-adults. This can happen for many reasons. The experience of being placed in an adult role as a child has far-reaching effects that can change the course of a person's life—even multiples decades after the experience occurred.

In an ideal world, people who have children would have left their own childhoods with their mental health, sense of self-esteem, and ability to navigate healthy relationships intact. They would then parent their own children with that same healthy sense of connection, individuality, and social responsibility, appropriate to their ages and maturity levels. But as anyone reading this book knows, we do not live in a perfect society where all adults are walking around undamaged. Because of that, many people who have really positive intentions in raising healthy and loved children still struggle with the boundaries of the parent-child relationship.

Consider a single mom who grew up in an alcoholic, abusive home that she left at a young age to escape the violence. As a child, she swore up and down she would never do to her children what was done to her—she would never be *her* parents. She was serious in her intentions to do the right thing.

She gets a job, tries to change her life, and has kids of her own. But because of a lack of education and the traumas she grew up with, she inadvertently chooses a partner to have children with who is just as abusive as her father or mother were to her. She can't believe she fell into the same old traps in her own relationship, but she finds a way out. Gets two jobs. Finds a way to raise her kids independently.

But now she is afraid. She left one abusive situation and found another. This mom no longer believes she can have a partner, or that she knows how to have a healthy relationship. She is working all the time. She is unable to spend time with like-minded peers because when she isn't working, she is with her children. As time goes on, she starts to get super sad and lonely but she stuffs it down, because she has to just roll up her sleeves and get by. Because she is lonely and isn't getting any mental health support—due to a lack of time, resources, and money—and she isn't engaging with anyone else other than her colleagues, she starts to discuss things with her ten-year-old son that would really only be appropriate to share with another adult.

It could start with just talking about her day and the regular work stresses. She might see that he is 'okay' with that and begin to share other things, like her anxieties around her lack of dating, relationships, and even sex. Maybe over time, her need for physical touch goes unmet and she expects her son to cuddle with her, even past the age where it is appropriate for a child to cuddle with their parents. It all seems innocent enough; I mean, they are just cuddling with their clothes on.

**Note**: I'm not talking here about kids who ask to cuddle their parents and want to be close to them to meet their *own* needs. I'm referring to the parent who is so lacking in connection that they encourage their child to do these things, even when the child may feel uncomfortable, for the parent's own benefit. The difference is significant and important to recognize.

None of these behaviors are horrific in the same way as those by parents intentionally inflicting physical, sexual, mental, and/or emotional violence on their children, or by parents overtly ignoring these things happening to their child and not protecting them. However, that does not mean these subtle shifts in emotional responsibility are not extremely harmful to the child in the long run.

What is happening in this scenario? This parent had really great intentions. She wanted nothing more than to right the wrongs she had endured. And she tried really, really hard to change the course of her life. But, unfortunately, she is carrying the same trauma she grew up with and filtering it down to her son in a different way. This parent is shifting the attention and focus away from being a parent who is parenting the child—where the child is rightly never responsible for the parent's emotional, intellectual, or physical needs—to situating the child as the 'parent' to their own parent. In this situation, the child is being pushed to respond to the parent's emotional, intellectual, and physical needs.

What does this do to the child? First, the child may feel instantly uncomfortable while this is happening, but he has no frame of reference for what is normal outside of his one parent. He is also a kid, so he wants nothing more than to be loved and adored by his mother. Additionally, he doesn't trust his own intuition that this kind of role reversal isn't right—in fact, it kind of makes him feel special and important, and he likes again receiving some of the attention he lost after his younger sister was born. This 'unique' relationship he has with Mom makes him feel valued, seen, and maybe even like her 'favorite.' How could he not fall into that role?

What happens next? He starts to shy away from making deeper friendships at school because he starts to worry about his mom all day. He begins to feel responsible for her bad days at work, her loneliness, her lack of a dating life or friendships—and, for goodness' sake, all he wants to do is help and make it better. He rushes home from school before she gets home from work to have dinner on the table for everyone. He cleans up her messes after she eventually turns to alcohol to escape her ever-growing loneliness and fear of the future. He begins monitoring her every move to make sure she gets up for work on time and takes care of even her most basic needs.

As the child grows up, he isolates himself from social events on the weekends. When he does go out, he feels guilt, fear, and shame that his mom is still alone and he is out in the world having fun. His mom doesn't dissuade him from this guilt because she has become dependent on his support in her life.

He is a really good kid. He even gets lauded at school for his perfect behavior and grades. Being a perfect and 'mature' kid is really paying off for him! He may be exhausted from needing to be vigilant all the time, but he also notices the benefits. At this point, when even social validation for these behaviors start to emerge, he has fully become the Parentified Child—a child who is now more the parent emotionally than the parent is to him.

He has now also developed four key traits that will lead him into the next phase of his life:

- Being a helper or fixer of other people's problems (and doing it perfectly) in order to maintain a feeling of being special.
- Shame/guilt about having autonomy from his primary relationship.
- Feeling completely and totally responsible for other people's feelings.
- Expressing no needs or feelings of his own for fear he will be abandoned if he takes up too much space in relationships.

These four traits are the hallmark of the Parentified Child.

This young man now goes out into the world as overly emotionally responsible, empathic, and mature, yet totally unequipped with some of the most fundamental building blocks of what makes a life. He can listen like a champ, give advice, and show up immediately in a crisis, but he might not know how to make a real friend. When he should have been playing with his peers, he was supporting his mom, or organizing a bank account, or taking care of his own needs for physical, mental, and emotional well-being. He is now an adult who went to graduate school in life emotionally before he even got to kindergarten.

He goes out into the working world and dating world with a persona he must maintain in order to feel special and a secret to hide: that he literally only has one major tool for living, being a perfect caretaker of others in order to fit in. He does well at work but never gets promoted—he doesn't understand why, because he does ten times more than everyone else and stays at the office hours later than his co-workers. He doesn't get asked to go out after work by his colleagues because he doesn't know how to connect to them; they find him socially awkward. When he does go out, he can't stop thinking about what a terrible son he is for not being with his mom. He still calls his mom every night to check on her and stops by her house several days a week; he wants to check if her progressing drinking is 'manageable.'

He gets lucky and meets a woman at the local pub, where he eats alone most nights of the week. She is the bartender. She grew up with a horribly abusive father and the minute she meets him, she tells him her entire life story. He is instantly hooked—if a complete stranger trusted him enough to tell her his whole life story in the first thirty minutes of meeting, he must be "special." He makes decent money and has a perfectly tailored apartment, so he quickly rescues the bartender from her abusive home and into his.

But she drinks. She drinks a lot. She yells at him and even physically abuses him a few times. He sees this as a sign that he needs to love her more, give her more, and that she just needs him to be more supportive—then she will change. He begins the same cycle with her that he has long held with his mom: monitoring her drinking, feeling responsible for her pain, believing that he can somehow fix her wounds, and taking full responsibility for all the challenges in the relationship. He beats himself up for everything that doesn't go perfectly.

All through this, the real him is dying inside. He doesn't even know who the real him *is*, if he's honest with himself. His life becomes especially dark when the abusive, alcoholic bartender leaves him for another man, one who will abuse her and continue her cycle of self-loathing. He doesn't understand. He was *perfect*. He did everything he learned to do. He did all the things that were supposed to promise him everlasting love and support. But all it did was get him abandoned.

Shortly after that, his mom gets in a drunk-driving accident and doesn't survive.

He has a complete mental breakdown. He is convinced that if he'd gone to his mom's that night, he could have saved her life. Believing himself selfish and repulsive and worthless, he thinks he failed at his one purpose in life. This is all *his* fault. He has no ability to stand in his own skin without another person to take care of because that sense of autonomy was robbed from him starting at the age of ten. He is now thirty-four and literally at the bottom emotionally, mentally, and financially, because he gave his mother and girlfriend money that fed their addictions.

He is in a panic. He can't breathe. His entire sense of self and identity come crashing down. He turns to his younger sister to try to save her, but she doesn't need saving. She has taken a different path—she got help, went to a recovery program, and even formed a relationship with someone healthy and well-adjusted, who loves her unconditionally. She loves her brother, but she rejects his attempts to try to fix her because she just isn't broken any longer.

This is when he entirely crumbles. For the first time in his life, he has nobody to save. He also has no frame of reference for what life means when he isn't looking outside of himself to rescue another person. This wasn't his fault, after all; this is all he ever knew.

At this point, he is at a crossroads. He is either going to hit an emotional bottom and find the help he so desperately needs, or he is going to find the first person he can who will allow him to take over the role of rescuer/caregiver in their life. The choice is up to him. But hopefully, at this point, the pain is so great that he is willing to learn a new way of living: one that no longer feeds his sense of self-worth by existing solely to feed life to a weaker, more troubled person.

Maybe you can identify with some of the traits that either the mom or the son are coping with. Neither of these people were bad people; they just fell into bad and emotionally stilted patterns. Both needed help.

■ ■ ■

The same scenario could be applied to a different and more widely discussed form of childhood abuse: sexual abuse. Sexual connection is meant for consensual adults who have a solid understanding of their bodies and who know and can discuss what they like and don't like. These adults are equipped with a sense of emotional maturity that lends itself to managing and understanding what it means to be physically intimate with another person. When sexual molestation happens to children, that ability to decipher one's sexuality as autonomous dissipates.

To complicate the abhorrent nature and devastating ramifications of childhood sexual abuse, in most cases the person who sexualizes the child is a person they love, admire, and adore—and in many cases, someone they rely on for emotional and/or financial support. The abuser often 'romanticizes' the abusive relationship, which then creates a lifelong conflict for the victim. Painful and inappropriate relationships are made to feel like 'love' and healthy, safe, and supportive people—ones who would intervene to stop the abuse if they knew about it—are made to feel like 'enemies.'

Why might this be the case? Let's consider a child who is sexually abused by a parent, sibling, mentor, or caregiver. This adult figure gives her intermittent love and attention, and maybe even tells her the abuse happens because they have a 'special relationship.' The child undoubtedly knows there is something very wrong with this interaction, but her other caregiver(s) may be so self-absorbed or dissociated from their own pain that they don't pay any attention to her. This makes it appealing to have one parent, caregiver, or mentor who pays 'special attention' to her. Maybe this child is also very confused because, even though this relationship is supposedly 'special,' the abuser also threatens her, telling her very bad things will happen if she tells anyone about their relationship. The feeling of being loved becomes fused with abuse in her brain—connection and danger go together.

This child grows up and goes out into the world. Maybe she is a high achiever with lots of friends. Maybe she garners great success in her work life and is physically in great shape. Maybe she is even funny and relatable on the outside. But her friends can't help but notice that she only has sexual encounters with strangers—never people who are close—or she only has romantic relationships with people who are emotionally unavailable and/or who abuse her and eventually leave. They see potential partner after partner come along, people who want to be kind to her, show up for her, and be a friend as well as a romantic interest. But she shoves all of them as far away as humanly possible. She only seems to equate attraction and love with pain and abuse, which then confuses her even more because she starts to feel she is totally unlovable and unworthy of anything real.

What is the conflict here? This woman was robbed of her power of sexual choice. She was confused and mixed up by someone she loved and adored, who she thought was totally safe, and she was shamed into believing that love was also secrecy and punishment. She goes out into the world believing that what she wants is a healthy, loving relationship—but every time one comes along, she runs and pushes the person away. She cannot fathom having sex with someone who is nice, as someone who was 'nice' to her abused and destroyed her. If she has sex with people she doesn't care about or relationships with people who are mean, then she never really has to experience emotional vulnerability—she always has an out. Somewhere inside of her she knows that she picks people who will leave or hurt her so that she can avoid the feeling of being trapped. But, of course none of this ends up feeling good or working. And only serves to make her feel more mixed up inside.

What is the crisis here? In many ways, a person who is actualized as an autonomous, fully embodied adult is still acting out childhood trauma. What she *really* wants is love and support, but she doesn't know how to receive it. After years and years of watching her friends or acquaintances develop healthy and loving partnerships, she is in her middle life and all alone. She knows she cannot go back to abusers; she has done that, and it reached a point where it hurt more than it felt familiar. But she has no idea how to allow or receive something healthy, as that seems both boring and totally terrifying at the same time.

At this point, one of two things is going to happen. She will allow someone who is kind and consistent to show up and offer a safe, supportive relationship. No matter how uncomfortable that type of real connection feels, she will practice and take it one tiny step at a time. The second option is she will go back to the same old patterns that hurt and cause undue angst—not because she wants to, but because that feels like the only language she can understand.

As in the example of the boy with Parentified Child syndrome, she is also at a crossroads. However, what is really crucial to understand is that going after the loving relationship can actually be excruciatingly painful. It will require her to feel and deal with all the unmet trauma wounds that come to the surface when she is presented with authentic love and care.

There is a third option: that she will become shut down and just remain totally alone. That would be very sad, because that isn't what she wanted or hoped for in life. Change, in this case, would be the only choice to achieve happiness. That level of challenge and pain is something she would never have had to endure if her sexual freedom and childhood innocence had not been robbed from her when it was not her fault.

It is absolutely possible to heal from trauma wounds, including sexual trauma wounds. However, it requires an in-depth willingness to do so, and an amount of work that can be very painful and raw to experience. In this case, the survivor must decide if having something that feels healthy and good, and no longer feeling alone or abused, is worth the work involved. That is an individual choice that each survivor must make on their own.

When a child is robbed of the decision to choose with whom they experience their first sexual encounter, it is imperative to remember the following: The survivor always gets to decide how they will move forward. It is neither a failure nor a tragedy if the person who has endured sexual molestation chooses to avoid sexual encounters as a way to feel safe. While many trauma survivors will decide to work through their fears around sexual intimacy combined with emotional intimacy, it is absolutely not wrong for a person to decide that they simply cannot.

CHAPTER 6

# CHILDHOOD TRAUMA: THINGS TO LOOK OUT FOR

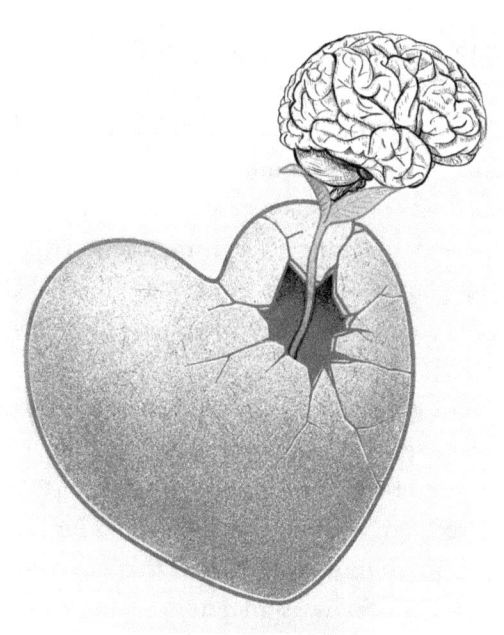

In the last chapter, we covered some of the nuanced ways childhood trauma manifests into one's adult life and relationships. The next step to understanding childhood trauma, and how to successfully navigate it with the people you love, is to look at typical response behaviors and offer practical suggestions for responding in the most effective ways possible.

## TYPICAL WAYS CHILDHOOD TRAUMA SHOWS UP IN DAILY LIFE

### *Extreme Sensitivity to Touch*

If you live with or work with someone who has experienced childhood trauma, you may notice that they show specific body language indicating they are 'shut down.' If the person was physically and/or sexually abused, touch can be very confusing for them. Perhaps they stand or sit at a distance from other people at group meetings, cringe if you put your hand on their shoulder unexpectedly, or physically turn away from others when they feel too close. When a child is sexually traumatized, this can alter their ability to distinguish more than one type of touch as different from a 'bad' touch; as a result, they may live in a world where unexpected touching is legitimately terrifying. This can hurt the safe people in their lives, particularly close friends or partners, because it can make them feel like they are doing something wrong.

Offering safe touch to the people you care about isn't wrong. However, it is crucial to understand that in order to be a safe person in the life of someone who has been abused, you need to learn to defer to them on touch and when and how often that can happen. The thing to remember here is that a freedom was taken from them as a child; now as an adult, having total control over that aspect of their life may be their only way to feel safe. This can be painful for people on the receiving end of these shutdowns or rigid rules, but it is nowhere near as painful as what your friend or loved one endured as a child.

**Some examples of shutting down to touch may include:**

- Jumping up or running away when unexpectedly touched.
- Showing body language indicating they have shut down, such as always having their arms crossed or their body turned away.
- Avoiding time with other people, especially during times of high stress.
- Positioning themselves at the far end of the table or away from other people during a meal, meeting, or conversation.
- Freezing up when a friend or partner tries to hug them.
- Picking fights, being mean, or distancing themselves from other people in ways that make them feel safe from their fear of too much physical or emotional closeness.
- Choosing to be around other people who have shut down, or who will either ignore them or administer abusive touch, as that is more familiar, even when it's painful.
- Cringing when someone tries to initiate a hug or any sort of physical contact over which they do not feel in control.

These are only a few typical responses to a fear of touch for a childhood trauma survivor, and they certainly are not universal. Every person reacts differently to trauma yet has a similar pain that they carry inside. But if you can be sensitive to the fact that most childhood abuse survivors need to know they have a choice in being touched or not, that can position you as a much safer person in their life. It can also help you understand that this situation isn't something you caused, and it is not intended as a direct rejection against you and your care. Patience, space, and understanding are key.

**Some recommendations for accommodations:**

- Let them initiate most physical contact.
- Talk to them when they are in a good space mentally about what feels safe for them and doesn't. If that makes them uncomfortable, say you can talk about it at another time.
- Affirm you are safe with consistent actions, as well as consistent respect of their physical boundaries.
- If you feel hurt or rejected by the person physically, only initiate conversation about this when the person is not already triggered.
- Never use physical touch in any way to hurt the other person.
- Model respect for your own physical boundaries and remain consistent with them.
- If this person has shared their story with you, make sure they know you will not breach that confidence by disrespecting their boundaries and sharing their story with someone else.
- Lovingly point out their tendency to close off when you are close, and remind them you will never ever intentionally hurt them.
- Be emotionally and mentally consistent.
- Keep your promises.
- Respect physical and emotional boundaries, especially if you have already discussed these with the person and asked them directly about their needs.

**Note**: One important thing to remember about childhood trauma is that most of the time, the majority of it was shoved under the proverbial rug. Openly talking about feelings and needs can feel like ripping off skin; it can be so uncomfortable for a childhood trauma survivor. So patience, space, and understanding are integral. The person needs to know that if they ever need space from you, or need to share that something you do makes them uncomfortable, that it is okay.

These accommodations can take a lot of work, but they are worth making if you truly care about the childhood trauma survivors in your life. We all have challenges, and we all need additional support sometimes. The more you can share that support with the people you care about that are hurting in this way, the safer they can feel in the world around them, as well as in relation to you.

An important thing to remember is that while it is vital to be respectful and patient, it is not okay for you to leave all your needs unmet in an effort to make the other person comfortable. As with all accommodations, make sure to communicate how the other person's shutting down makes you feel while remaining open to hearing what the fear of closeness feels like for them. If someone you care about has totally shut down and it is repeatedly hurtful to you, it may be time to talk to them about what they are willing to do on their end to get the professional support and healing that would help them be open and connected.

### *Push/Pull Responses*

When a child grows up with trauma, they are likely very confused about the nature of what consistent and healthy connection looks and feels like. In many dysfunctional and unsafe families, children experience intermittent positive reinforcement (attention, love, validation) interspersed with abuse. This creates a very perplexing relationship to the world for the child, as it makes them feel a connection they enjoy and are equally terrified of simultaneously.

What tends to happen when a child is exposed to this inconsistent reinforcement of both love and pain/abuse is that they learn that they can desire connection, but they can never truly have it in a sustainable way. This mixed-up orientation to the world attracts more abusers to this person because that back-and-forth response from a partner or friend is something they find familiar and even attractive. It also makes them push/pull this way themselves with the safe people who show up in their lives.

Because of this confusion, childhood trauma survivors often find themselves stuck in relationships that are painful, and running from relationships that are good. This is so ingrained that the childhood trauma survivor will even subconsciously try to recreate the push/pull pain with safe people by doing it so much themselves that they eventually push those people away. This gives them the chance to say, "See, I knew I was unlovable!" when that wasn't at all what was happening. What was happening was that 'mean people' felt safe and 'safe people' felt terrifying. Therefore, they clung to the mean and sabotaged their connection to the safe.

If a person in your life who has endured childhood trauma is behaving in ways where they come close and then go away, it *is* possible to grow together, both as friends and family members. However, it will require extreme patience and a lot of unconditional love—for both yourself and them.

**Some examples of how push/pull responses show up in childhood trauma survivors:**

- Being available often until the other person comes 'too close,' then backing away or behaving in avoidant or confusing ways.
- Making, and then canceling, plans regularly. Even pretending like the plans were never talked about or made.

## CHILDHOOD TRAUMA: THINGS TO LOOK OUT FOR

- Having outbursts of anger, fighting, or rejecting behaviors when things feel 'too good' or 'too close.'
- Showing up full throttle at work, then missing a bunch of days, coming in late, or being distracted during meetings.
- Being there, but not being present. In other words, being in the same room but not seeming present or responding to most of what people say—effectively, responding from a place of dissociation.
- Being very engaged for a period of time, then disengaged, then engaged, then disengaged (and much more engaged when the other party starts to pull away).

Being connected to someone who reacts in these ways can be very painful, especially if you have a history of childhood trauma yourself. Because of that, it is important to remember that compassion is key, but accepting abuse is not. If the person tries to be aware of these patterns, acknowledges them, and apologizes when appropriate, that is a good sign. It is very hard to heal from abuse injuries, and the people in your life with these challenges will need your patience and understanding in order to trust you in the long term.

**Some recommended accommodations for the survivor:**

- Let them come and go as they need to while making sure your needs are met in other situations and other ways that are productive.
- Make sure they know that you are not upset with them for their challenges, but hold them accountable if and when their actions hurt.
- Remember that, generally speaking, if someone behaves this way, they are feeling vulnerable and afraid—their reaction is

not directed toward you. Knowing this will allow you to not fight back, not blame them, and not cling to them when they need their own space to reground.
- Be respectful of obvious boundaries while also setting your own for what you will and will not tolerate.
- Let them know that you are there for them, even when they don't acknowledge or respond that you are saying it. They hear you; they are just afraid to accept it sometimes, for fear that it might hurt or go away.

It is important to note that these periods of push/pull may never entirely go away, but they should improve over time. It will be crucial for you, as someone who cares about a childhood trauma survivor, to not take their behavior personally. You need to remember that their actions are coming from their own inner conflict and not something you have or have not done, especially if you are doing your best to be reliable, consistent, and safe.

## *Self-Sabotage*

When a child is subjected to pain, they can grow up feeling shameful, secretive, and totally unworthy. This is so unfair because, had the same child been reared in a safe and loving home, they would not have had to endure this challenge throughout life. What often happens to a child who grows up feeling like they are bad or a 'mistake' is that they tend to sabotage positive things as soon as they feel 'too good'. This is really confusing for a trauma survivor, because all they wanted as a child was to feel safe and good. But things that feel too good are scary because they bring up feelings of vulnerability and openness.

When do you think these children were most damaged during the abuse cycles in their homes? It was during periods of openness and extreme vulnerability. For an adult who experienced childhood trauma to learn they are safe to expect and navigate good things in their lives, it is important to help them take goodness in incremental doses. They need to build a tolerance for feeling good in the right situations to believe it is absolutely safe and okay.

**Some examples of self-sabotage that can show up in childhood trauma survivors:**

- Getting excited about new things, only to quit them or shove them away once feelings of exposure and vulnerability start to surface.
- Refusal to take compliments or credit, or even allow themselves positive thoughts, for the many things they do well.
- Inviting people close who will mirror their perceived worthlessness while pushing away people who honor their true goodness, value, and worth, then pining for the kind people once they leave and move on.
- Constant busyness that doesn't allow anyone to get close.
- Negative behavior patterns that keep anyone who may get remotely close away, or blow up any success that may feel too good.
- Self-abandonment through poor diet, emotional withdrawal, addictions, self-loathing, and/or extreme isolation.

**Some recommended accommodations:**

- Provide support to the person, no matter what type of day or feeling they are having. If they feel worthless, listen; and if they feel good, remind them that they are worthy of that feeling.
- Don't shove toxic positivity down their throat by insisting they always be in a good mood or always feel hopeful.

- Offer supportive suggestions that reflect that you see they may be self-sabotaging, but aren't blaming them for it.
- Encourage them to learn to accept positive life experiences by degrees of tolerance. Ask them, "How much feeling 'worthy' or 'receiving' can you tolerate today?" and show support that feels safe to them.
- Avoid colloquialisms that minimize their fears and make light of their anxieties.

Childhood trauma survivors are often taught that to dream is to die. Almost every time they garnered some hope, something bad may have happened in the home. Maybe they were also told they were worthless, and to dream would mean receiving more rejection. In order for a childhood trauma survivor to feel safe to have hope again, they need measurable support that is both reliable and consistent. They also need reflections of their strengths in ways that make sense, not in ways that feel like more pressure.

## CHILDHOOD TRAUMA: THINGS TO LOOK OUT FOR

### CALL TO ACTION

Take out your list again; get more paper, if needed. What, if any, of the above behaviors have you noticed in either yourself or others as a result of experiencing childhood trauma? Think about those behaviors. First, spend some time journaling about what you or your loved one(s) have done *right* in response to these challenges. Then, spend some time giving yourself credit for the things that you didn't even realize you already knew.

If you are the person who has experienced the traumatic event(s), how might communicating some of what you learned above to your closest people help you feel more supported? How might that make you feel vulnerable and scared? If you love someone who has experienced these things, how can you continue to learn and grow so that you can be more supportive and take their reactions less personally?

Take a little time to reflect on the last two chapters. As always, if any feelings that are too painful arise, it is always okay to take a break and put this book down. Just keep reminding yourself that you don't have to do anything you aren't ready for or don't want to do. These are all supportive suggestions, not adamant directives or declarations.

CHAPTER 7

# AMBIGUOUS TRAUMA AND HOW IT IMPACTS OUR LIVES

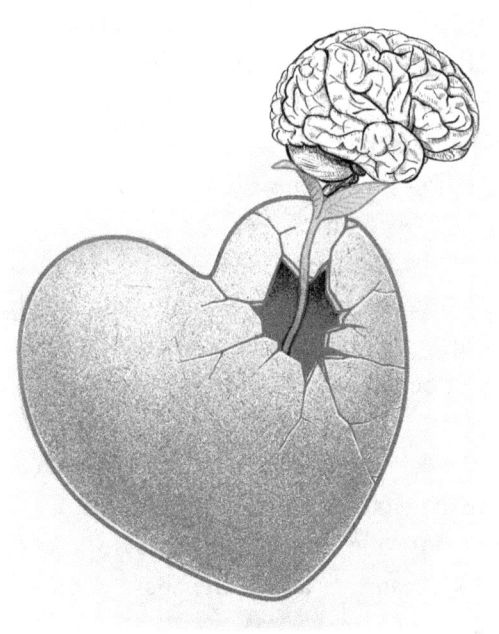

Ambiguous trauma is trauma that involves a person or situation that abruptly, gradually, or unexpectedly changes, but one that we have repeated exposure to in ways that cause pain and heartbreak as things unfold. Ambiguous trauma is ongoing and most often includes a sense of grief that feels hard to ever let go of for the person experiencing it.

Unlike the other four main types of trauma I identify in this book, ambiguous trauma is rarely discussed. The very nature of this type of trauma is that it can often seem elusive, confusing, and hard to even communicate. Additionally, while all forms of trauma create a funnel of grief and loss within us, ambiguous trauma impacts us in a way that is deeply confusing to understand, process, and heal.

**Some examples of things that can cause ambiguous trauma:**

- Traumatic brain injury of yourself or a loved one.
- Stroke/heart attack or other medical crisis that creates a changed personality in yourself or a loved one.
- Addiction in yourself or a loved one.
- Loss of vision or hearing, or a loss of physical aptitude, of yourself or a loved one.
- Onset or recurrence of mental illness in yourself or a loved one.
- Change in dynamic of a relationship with family, a friend, or a significant other, where the change is recurring or ongoing and cannot be adequately addressed through conversation or processing.
- Return of a loved one from combat with a changed physical and/or mental state of being.
- Long-term loss of work, or inability to do tasks that were once easy to do, because of any of the above and/or other medical or mental crises.

As you can see from the examples, ambiguous trauma involves something being one way, then another way, with no ability to change the new way even though it hurts.

■ ■ ■

Let's consider the spouse of a man who has a severe accident. This couple met in high school. They are best friends, he is her life partner, and they parent four kids. These two have been married for 24 years and, despite some normal life vicissitudes, have really maintained their feelings of happiness, connection, support, fun, and love. They both have solid careers, a supportive extended family network, and some really amazing friends. Their kids are healthy and faring well in life.

One day on the husband's way to work, he is hit by a person driving a semi who is texting while driving. At first, everyone is beyond thrilled that their father/brother/partner/friend survived the terrible accident despite the heavy damage to his car. In the days after the accident, the man is in a coma; everyone is just hoping and praying that he will wake up. When he does, it is a time of rejoicing.

However, what becomes clear in the days and weeks following the tragic accident is that he (let's call him Bill) is not the same person he was before. The damage to his brain didn't cause death or even a vegetative state of being; however, it was substantial enough to cause a traumatic brain injury that has fundamentally changed him.

Bill was once quick on his feet, fun, and able to focus with a memory that almost no one could match; now, he speaks very slowly, can't comprehend most jokes, and forgets how to do small and basic tasks. Prior to the accident, Bill was very patient—the most calming force in his family. Unfortunately, in addition to losing some basic and typical cognitive functioning for a person his age, Bill now also has a very short frustration tolerance—in part because he is traumatized by not being able to do the things he used to be able to do—and sometimes even yells at his kids and his wife.

Essentially, what happened is that Bill left that day for work as a partner, father, and friend and returned as a stranger.

Now, what is his spouse to do? She met him when they were only kids. The Bill she knew was absolutely the love of her life. She promised him she would be there in sickness and in health, yet now she is trapped in a house with a person she loves physically but doesn't know anymore.

Additionally, Bill can no longer work his job because he cannot complete the mental tasks required. He was given a healthy severance and early retirement, so money isn't a real problem for the family. However, now that Bill is home all day he is becoming more and more despondent and depressed, as he is also experiencing the trauma of not knowing himself anymore. Bill's kids are equally devastated and confused, as their father, who once made them laugh with glee and was there to support them at life's every twist and turn, has grown withdrawn, aloof, and depressed.

Everyone in the house essentially feels like Bill is 'walking dead,' but nobody can say anything for fear that Bill will be angry, feel rejected, and hurt even more than he does.

Bill's wife went from being a partner to essentially being a parent to a fifth child. She never plans to leave Bill, but now she must prepare for a life with a far less than equitable partnership. She is only 48. She thought they had their entire idyllic life left ahead of them but it turns out, they didn't. One morning, a man behind the wheel of a semi who decided to text while driving changed all that.

This situation constitutes ambiguous trauma for Bill, as well as all of his family and loved ones, because he will most likely never be the same as he was before. Even if he makes progress with his occupational therapy, he will still always have some sort of delayed response. He will never again be the person his wife fell in love with or his children grew so fond of and attached to during their younger years.

The nature of this trauma is that Bill is there, but Bill is also not there. His body and his appearance are the same—which shocked everyone, as the accident was so severe—but his way of being in the world is not. This type of trauma continues throughout, potentially, the course of the lives of everyone who loves Bill, and through his own life, and brings up feelings of grief and heartache at every first event, at every change, and at every time where the differences are glaringly obvious.

While the family and Bill will eventually adjust, it simply was not his wife's life dream to have a partner who presented as more of a child.

We can all read this and say, "Well, that is love, and we stick by people we love," or "That is just life." But until you experience this type of trauma, you simply cannot understand how absolutely devastating it is—not only due to the original event, but in the way it never ceases to reverberate.

It is very hard to grieve this type of loss and pain as it continues to hurt over and over again. While acceptance and resolve can absolutely occur over time, it is essential both for those dealing directly with the trauma to identify what it is and how it feels, and for their loved ones to support them in recognizing how devastating this all is.

■ ■ ■

Now let's look at ambiguous loss through a different lens. What if the person was physically there, but then, physically not there due to incarceration?

Imagine that a man had been a single father for years. He worked diligently to help his kids have better than he had. He even forewent fun and romance to work two jobs, be home at night to cook dinner, and make sure his kids never went to sleep alone as he had as a child.

As she grows up, this man's daughter really takes off. She goes to college, gets a job, and finds a soulmate— all the things that would help her single dad of two kids not worry about her. But his son was hypersensitive as a child. Because he was older, he remembered his mom more than the younger sister did—and he felt wholly abandoned when she left his father for another man, left the country, and never contacted them again. This crushed his little soul. Even though he loved his father and knew his father loved and cared for him unconditionally, he could never quite heal the pain of feeling like he wasn't 'good enough' to keep his mom around.

As the son gets older, he finds himself attracted to women who are either emotionally unavailable in some way or into hard drugs. As a young adult, he becomes attached to a woman who is not only addicted to meth but also sells it. He hangs out in drug houses with her, just so he can keep an eye on her—and so that he doesn't have to fear she will leave him as his mom did. Unfortunately, none of his father's pleading works and one night after a drug bust, he is arrested for possession, use, and sale of crystal meth. Due to his choices and being in the proverbial wrong place at the wrong time, the son is convicted and gets a prison sentence of multiple years.

What is the ambiguous grief in this case? The father is devastated and blames himself. He did everything he could to make up for the kids' mom abandoning them, but it simply wasn't enough to heal his son's heartbreak. As a result, the father must now endure the devastation of what he sees as letting his son down, as well as heartache over both the physical loss of his son for a period of time and the hope of him having a better future than he had. He can feel good about where his daughter is in life, but this only adds to his guilt. What could he have done better? How might he have tried harder? Did he give her favoritism he wasn't aware of? As a parent who wanted to do nothing but right by his son, it's only natural that he would have these feelings.

The sister also experiences ambiguous grief. She adores her older brother and misses him. She, too, has sleepless nights worrying about her brother in prison. Is he scared? Is he alone? Does he know they still love him?

This type of ambiguous trauma, while different from the loss in the example of the traumatic brain injury, is palpable, raw, and real. It leaves the father and sister heartbroken, not only because their family member is suffering and physically gone for the time being, but also because, at least for now, he is far from reaching his full potential.

It's possible that this young man will get sober in prison, get his act together, be released, and live a different life in the future. Nobody can know the outcome of the situation just yet. Additionally the trauma of lost time will affect them all—and when time is taken from us, that is a grief we can feel in some way for the rest of our lives.

There is hope here that this situation could completely turn around at some point. But for now, the pain everyone is feeling in this situation is real and must be acknowledged, addressed, and supported if any recovery is going to be possible.

■ ■ ■

As you can see with these examples of ambiguous trauma, this is a pain that echoes on and on from the time of onset. This type of trauma continues to impact the people involved over weeks, months, years, and sometimes even decades. For this reason, people experiencing ambiguous trauma often need ongoing professional and communal support.

CHAPTER 8

# AMBIGUOUS TRAUMA: THINGS TO LOOK OUT FOR

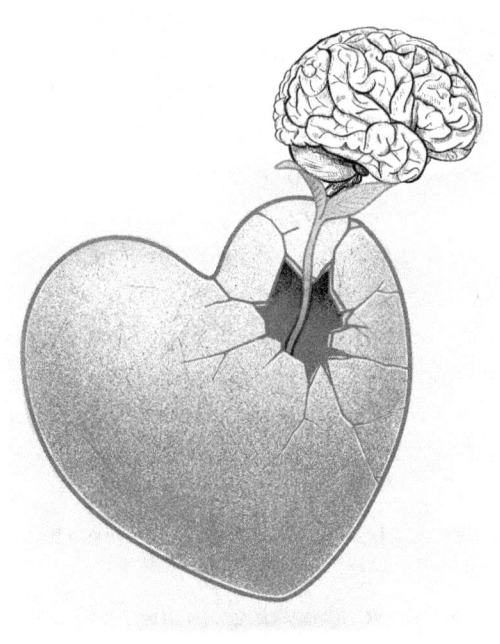

We have covered the basics about what ambiguous trauma is, what it feels like, and how it can be experienced by different people. Now let's take a closer look at how it shows up in one's daily life, and how supportive professionals and loved ones can help the person experiencing this trauma navigate it—and potentially heal from it.

## TYPICAL WAYS AMBIGUOUS TRAUMA SHOWS UP IN DAILY LIFE

### *Dissociation/Forgetfulness*

If you know someone experiencing ambiguous trauma, you may notice a dramatic shift in their ability to focus, especially compared to their abilities before the traumatic event. Depression that can lead to dissociation is one of the symptoms of trauma, especially when that trauma is ongoing.

To help you understand this a bit better, let's recall the example of the woman with kids whose husband had a brain injury. She could once trust that her spouse would manage half of the life they had built together, but now she must manage it all alone. Additionally, she is often preoccupied with worries about her husband's well-being and the mental and emotional health of their children. Sprinkled in with that is a healthy dose of anger at the person who caused the accident that injured her husband, and maybe even some anger at God or the universe for putting their family in this position.

Either way, she has *a lot* on her mind—and it is going to be very hard for her to be as acute and mentally "in the game" as she once was.

**Some examples of dissociation/forgetfulness that may occur:**

- Running late to work meetings, losing focus during meetings, and forgetting key points formerly recalled with ease.

## AMBIGUOUS TRAUMA: THINGS TO LOOK OUT FOR

- Frequently losing things like one's keys, forgetting where things are in the house or office, or forgetting purchases at the grocery store.
- Forgetting the special events of friends or loved ones.
- Forgetting one's destination while en route, or losing track of a conversation in the middle of it.
- Losing important papers or missing medical appointments or other important events without even realizing it.

These are just some examples of how dissociation/forgetfulness can show up in the life of someone coping with ambiguous trauma. There are certainly many more. However, if someone you care about is dealing with this there are things you can do to support them and help them adjust. Your support can also provide you a better chance of getting your own needs met in the relationship.

**Some recommendations for accommodations:**

- Remind the person to make lists and gently support them in doing so.
- Give them a heads-up if you have a special event or appointment coming up, and ask if they will have the mental space to attend.
- If they are a colleague, make sure you sit next to them at meetings to provide helpful prompts if needed.
- If they are your employee, give them extra time for tasks. Consider having a weekly check-in meeting to make sure they have everything they need to succeed at work in the coming days.
- Offer to help a friend or loved one with grocery shopping, cooking, school drop-off and pick-up, or at-home projects.
- Try to help them create time for self-care like medical appointments and physical care (hair, nails, shopping etc.).
- Show you care by doing simple things like showing up sometimes with snacks and a hug.

The thing to remember about people coping with ambiguous trauma is that they are *exhausted* and often feel very alone. When trauma is ongoing, most people tend to disperse and forget their loved one is suffering, but it's over time that things become worse. It is important to continue to check in, remain supportive, and replenish your own need for fun and self-care so that you don't become too drained while helping your loved one, colleague or friend cope with their trauma.

## *Anger Outbursts*

When someone is dealing with long-term ambiguous trauma, anger is normal. In many cases, the person feels isolated and forgotten by most people in their world, and the pain generally gets worse over time before it gets better.

What happens when someone feels drained and exhausted and alone? They get frustrated and angry. While we should never accept excessively loud or abusive outbursts toward us from those we care about, it is okay to allow a safe space for your loved one or friend to scream, cry, or express appropriately directed rage. Everyone needs to express those feelings sometimes. They need someone to listen to them and be a safe space for them if they are to heal.

**Some examples of how anger may show up in ambiguous trauma survivors:**

- Losing one's temper at something seemingly small.
- Being impatient with the one or two people who are kindest to, closest to, and always there for them.
- Road rage.
- Self injury like nail picking, biting, or hair pulling.

## AMBIGUOUS TRAUMA: THINGS TO LOOK OUT FOR

- Taking things more personally than usual and lashing out with lots of tears.
- Aggressively shutting doors, chopping food, or putting dishes away.
- Being mad at the person who is the focus of their trauma, such as an accident victim or incarcerated child.

It can be very hard to watch someone you care about become more aggressive because of their pain. When you feel like you don't recognize your friend or loved one anymore, that can be a secondary loss. That said, as hard as it is for you to see them this way, it is much harder for them to have to live with ambiguous trauma and grief. If you can work to be a safe space for someone coping with this type of trauma, while protecting your own heart and feelings, it can make a massive difference in this person's life.

**Some recommended accommodations for the survivors:**

- Let them know you are always there if they need to share big feelings, that those feelings are safe with you, and that you can handle them. Note: only say that if it is true for you.
- Make sure they know you notice their aggressive behaviors and that you wonder if they need to vent, go for a walk, or spend a night out on the town.
- Be someone who doesn't disappear from their life over time as the trauma continues. Remember that most people fade out of the survivor's life a few weeks or months after a trauma or a loss. You will stand out as a supporter if you commit to being there long-term.
- Give them space when they are in a particularly dark place, but let them know you are just a phone call away when they are ready to talk.

Once your friend, colleague, or loved one has really integrated this ambiguous trauma, things will get better. They will improve more quickly if they know you are there to help. However, if the rage they express gets out of hand, share your concern for their mental well-being and recommend they get professional help.

## *Self-Loathing/Blame*

When we experience a massive hurt in life—especially one like ambiguous trauma that leaves us feeling wholly out of control—it is very natural to blame ourselves. In some odd way, self-blame gives us the illusion of control, even when we have none. Additionally, self-blame is very common when things like accidents, incarceration, or addiction occur, because these situations often leave loved ones wondering "what if."

**Some examples of self-loathing/blame:**

- Feeling continuously guilty for not doing enough to save the person who experienced the accident, illness, legal consequences, or mental breakdown.
- Recurrent thoughts like "If I hadn't made him take the car that day, the accident wouldn't have happened," or "If I hadn't let him be exposed to my addict mother, he wouldn't have become addicted to drugs"—the list goes on. As with ambiguous trauma, there is often not a clear-cut reason for the situation. It is vague, and that is part of why it hurts so deeply.
- Feeling terrible survivor's guilt.
- Staying "stuck" in life for fear that if they move forward, they may hurt the person suffering or miss the opportunity to change things, even if the situation is unchangeable.
- Numbing out with food, work, television, gambling—anything to distract from their pain.

- Avoiding people who could be supportive to constantly sit in one's pain and sorrow instead.
- Feeling guilt about being angry at the focus of their trauma.

**Some recommended accommodations:**

- Help the person recognize that no matter how many times they play the "what if" game, they will never get a solid answer—sometimes life is unfair and we cannot know or predict how things will land.
- Listen to their feelings, but also gently guide them back to reality with reminders such as "Car accidents we don't cause are never our fault," "Sometimes terrible things happen and it hurts," or "It is so hard to not be able to plan or know when these awful things in life will occur. It has to feel so tragic to not know if it could have been different." These are reflective comments that don't diminish a person's feelings, but also don't feed into self-loathing.
- Help them make a list of the things they *do* have control over and encourage them to focus on those.
- Make a list of facts that remind them what is actually true about how this situation evolved. Encourage them to look at these facts when they get too deep into self-loathing feelings.

Every day, we're surrounded by people coping with ambiguous trauma. They are our friends, colleagues, neighbors, and clergy members, and they are also the strangers walking by us in the mall. This type of trauma is very common, yet still so often unaddressed and misunderstood. In fact, just reading the last two chapters on this topic puts you ten steps ahead of most in understanding either your own or someone else's struggle with ambiguous trauma. That knowledge doesn't replace the obvious need for professional help in these situations, but taking the time to learn does arm you with more empathy and tools than you previously had.

> ## CALL TO ACTION
>
> Take out your list again. You may be very surprised at how little on your list was related to ambiguous trauma. If you were to add to your list, what things that either you or people you know are dealing with that could be ambiguous trauma? Which behaviors have you noticed, in either yourself or others, that need to be addressed? Which of the suggested accommodations are you willing to try?
>
> Take a little time to reflect on the last two chapters. If you feel triggered, take a break or a pause. There is no rush to learn this stuff or become an "expert." Even trying to understand ambiguous trauma and be there for those who you know are coping with it is a remarkable step in the right direction. Because ambiguous trauma can be so nuanced, I recommend reading the last two chapters a few times before you start to attempt the accommodations. Also, remain patient with yourself as you learn how to be a bigger support to others—and to yourself in this process.

# CHAPTER 9

# WORKPLACE TRAUMA AND HOW IT IMPACTS OUR LIVES

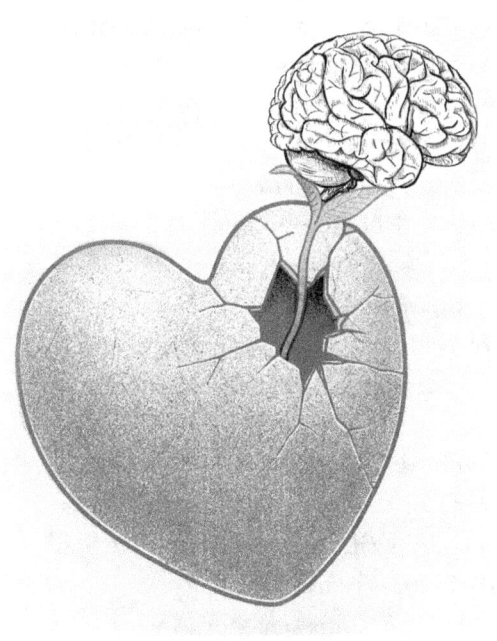

In the overview of the main categories of trauma, I mentioned different types of workplace trauma, which we'll discuss in more detail in this chapter. This type of trauma can be difficult to tease out because workplace trauma happens all over the world daily. Some types of workplace trauma are particularly difficult because they can mirror childhood trauma experiences. For example, a raging or controlling boss might mirror a raging and controlling parent, or a situation where one feels they can't ever win or succeed could bring up childhood struggles with perfectionism. However, regardless of one's experience with childhood trauma, workplace trauma can happen independently and have a very strong impact on a person's life.

One of the better-known forms of workplace trauma is that experienced by many veterans who come back from combat zones. These people have an entirely different lens through which they see the world and evaluate safety, and they sometimes don't know how to fit into a place that isn't a literal warzone. This type of trauma is one where the job itself is a hazard to one's mental health.

The difference between this type of workplace trauma and one that is more relationally based is that someone in the military is aware that traumatic experiences are inevitable in combat. In contrast, a person who goes to work everyday in a corporate setting doesn't necessarily expect a scenario like a narcissistic boss who belittles them at every turn, to give one example of a potential source of trauma. The same situation applies if their boss is a bigot who undermines their success and attempts to always be in control.

I make this distinction not to minimize the tragedy that befalls veterans in any way. Veteran trauma is so complex and tragic, that I could write an entirely separate book just about that. However, it is important to distinguish between the different types of workplace trauma and how, in many cases, this trauma comes seemingly out of nowhere, as opposed to trauma that is a known hazard in a particular line of work.

■ ■ ■

To discuss workplace trauma, let's focus on the less discussed type: emotional and mental trauma in the workplace. Let's say there is a woman who gets a new job at a company and is entirely enthusiastic about her new opportunity. Let's also say this woman has always been a top performer in both school and work settings. A standout person, she was used to getting straight As and the approval of her mentors. She is kind to others, follows guidelines, and is great as a team player. She even attended an Ivy League school, where she was also successful.

After college, she got a high-paying consulting job. Her boss was a woman who, upon hiring her, seemed like an authentic, engaged, and supportive leader. But the woman doesn't know is that the new manager had a very abusive childhood. The manager's father was a cruel, diminishing man who required perfection at all costs. While the new employee received praise and good grades effortlessly, in her youth her boss did not. All the boss ever wanted was approval from her father, and she didn't understand that it was impossible to get.

The boss showed her best self during the interview process, but the nuanced and underlying issues related to her childhood trauma soon come to the surface. Due to her father's abuse, the manager now has a competitive edge—she feels threatened by anyone more talented, more successful, or more likable than she believes herself to be. Even though she is very astute at projecting confidence, inside she is deeply self-loathing and insecure.

The manager hired her new colleague with seemingly good intentions, but without personal accountability or awareness.

And soon enough, her new team member's immediate success and likeability triggers in the manager both a fierce anxiety and a deeply troubling competitive nature.

Focusing in on the word 'competition' helps us understand how complicated this scenario is. Remember, this manager is supposed to be her employee's mentor, not her competitor. She should be focused on mentorship, guidance, setting up areas and opportunities for success, and listening to and learning from her new colleague. But because of her own childhood wounds around perfectionism and feeling unworthy, she immediately feels threatened by her bright new employee. The new hire is not only fast on her feet and an amazing asset to the team, but she is also almost immediately adored and validated by everyone in the department.

The new employee isn't trying to compete with her boss. She's just trying to be herself, impress her team, and do a great job. A healthy boss would see this woman as an asset. A toxic boss with unexamined trauma will see her as a threat. This employee's amazing nature triggers her manager's non-existent self-worth and fear of not being good enough.

After a few months of pretending to be a supportive mentor, the boss finds herself doing bizarre things to her employee: pretending she forgets parts of their conversations; falsely telling her she is making errors on documents for clients when it's just a matter of difference of opinion; and going around her and talking to consulting clients assigned to her without addressing her employee first. Not only are these forms of gaslighting, but these toxic behaviors also function to make the boss feel more powerful and less threatened. At the same time, they make the employee feel very stressed out and confused.

People who don't feel small to begin with don't need to feel bigger than their team. Through her attempts to feel less insecure, the boss begins to negatively impact and undermine her employee, who was initially so happy, eager, and open-minded about this new job.

Initially, the young woman is stumped. As time goes on, she starts to feel like there is nothing she can do correctly and like she has to constantly walk on eggshells at work. Despite the fact that she has always been successful, the boss she looks up to questions her abilities left and right. Over time, she begins to question her own judgment. The new employee has no prior history of substantial trauma, but she begins to feel triggered herself and starts having anxiety attacks before going to the office every day. She grows increasingly afraid of messing up, even though she was never really messing up to begin with. She also notices that nobody else at work is being treated this way, so she starts to wonder if *maybe she really is doing something wrong* that she is not seeing.

Keep in mind that this employee has no idea that her boss is deeply insecure and acting out of her own self-hate. Instead, she starts to blame herself. What do you think her boss does? The more the employee doubts herself, the more this feeds into her boss' desire to feel in control. And the more power it makes her boss feel, the more the boss doubles down on her criticism.

This dynamic creates a push-pull scenario where the employee falls deeply into feeling less and less capable. She starts to become unable to sleep and increasingly anxious around every area of her work. She also feels like she is not good enough and begins to lose self-esteem. The team member then starts to notice these new insecurities seeping into other areas of her life. This trauma at work is fueling a pattern of anxiety and pain around being treated as less than equal and a fear of getting in trouble.

The manager is clearly reacting to her own deep-rooted issues, but that doesn't make any difference. As the leader in her department, she should work on herself instead of taking out her unresolved trauma(s) on her employees. More importantly, she has no right to treat her colleague this way. Through her poor behavioral choices, she is causing serious damage to another human being.

Meanwhile, the young employee begins to unravel. Everything she thought about her own intellect and worth is being called into question. When other people suggest that it must be her boss who is the problem—that perhaps her boss is insecure or a control freak—she refuses to see it. She is so used to everyone loving her (because she is lovable) that she believes this shift in things must all be due to something glaringly wrong with her.

Over time, the employee becomes severely depressed. She seeks out support from a therapist, who almost immediately identifies the situation; but by now, the damage has been done. This woman, who once had a pretty darn solid sense of self-esteem, is now confused, panicked, and terrified almost every day of the week. She over analyzes everything she says and writes, for fear that her boss will diminish it. She is afraid of getting fired but equally afraid of looking for a new job—if she really is this incompetent, how could she possibly succeed anywhere else?.

At this point, one of a few things will happen. Through the help of the seasoned professional she already sought out, the woman will identify her boss as an emotional predator and a probable abuser acting out her own pain and ignorance. She will learn that these kinds of bosses are toxic, and that her manager's noxious behavior is not a reflection of her worth. If her manager is not held accountable, she may, unfortunately, have to start looking for a new, safer job where her contributions are celebrated. She will also need to work on signs to look out for in future managers, and she will begin the work of healing the trauma she has now experienced.

However, when she gets a new job she will likely need continued mental health support to avoid the cycle of thinking every manager or colleague has ill intent toward her. She must also learn that while other people's bad behavior can and has certainly impacted her life, it is never her fault.

How about the boss? Doesn't she need help too? Yes, she absolutely does. But in order for her to be able to receive help, she must realize there is some sort of problem. Either that or someone would have to go to human resources to complain about her unacceptable behavior, and she would ideally receive consequences for her actions and be recommended for some sort of training or therapy.

What most work environments will not be savvy enough to do, however, is identify this boss' behavior as a trauma response and treat it accordingly. If she gets reported, she will most likely either have the claims dismissed, or she will be written up and given consequences. However, she probably won't get any support for the emotional trauma from which her problems originated.

An organization that was sophisticated in Trauma Intelligence would encourage mental health support and an action plan to help the manager and the employee move past this challenging situation. There would also be guidelines established that ensured a safe space for the employee and success opportunities for the manager's improvement. If those changes were not actualized, then the organization would need to move forward with terminating the toxic boss.

■ ■ ■

How about a different but common workplace trauma—one related to the frontline workers during the COVID-19 pandemic? These professionals trained extensively to help others survive, but they had literally *no* training on how to respond to and function in the midst of a pandemic. They could never have adequately prepared for what came out of nowhere and landed with a crash.

This example of workplace trauma is crucial to understand, as it shows us that even when someone is fully trained in crisis and medical response, things can still occur that are out of everyone's hands. These situations can lead to unprepared emotional and physical reactions that lead to serious forms of post-traumatic stress disorder (PTSD).

If you or anyone you know has been a frontline worker during the pandemic, you will understand this tragedy firsthand. The crucial thing to recognize and understand in this situation is that, even when we are trained and prepared for hard things in the workplace, there is also the possibility of an outside, unexpected circumstance for which we are totally unprepared.

Many traumas in life are labeled such due in part to their unpredictable nature. This is the case for the frontline workers of the COVID-19 pandemic. Not only was there no preparation for what was to come, but there were also no shared languages or previous experiences with which to relate.

As humans, we look for feelings that relate to previous ones in order to process and understand lived experiences. One thing that helps a person heal from trauma is the ability to relate one feeling that is painful to a previous painful feeling that was effectively processed. When there is no previous language or recovery that is relatable to a person—as in the case of the pandemic—that makes both the trauma and healing from it even more difficult to endure.

In short, the world has now experienced an unexpected event that has created a whole new realm of workplace trauma that must be understood and addressed.

■ ■ ■

These are two examples of workplace trauma. There are myriad others that would be applicable here. While we work for the majority of our lives, most workplaces are highly under-resourced when it comes to the importance of Trauma Intelligence and support in the workplace. This lack of education and responsiveness is even true in work settings where trauma is an expected part of the work tasks themselves.

Just through reading this chapter, you are way ahead of the majority of people when it comes to an awareness of and desire to further understand workplace trauma and the very serious effects it can have on mental health. A good starting place may be to share this book or this chapter, or to begin a dialogue with a leader or a trusted colleague at work about trauma accountability and education in your organization.

CHAPTER 10

# WORKPLACE TRAUMA: THINGS TO LOOK OUT FOR

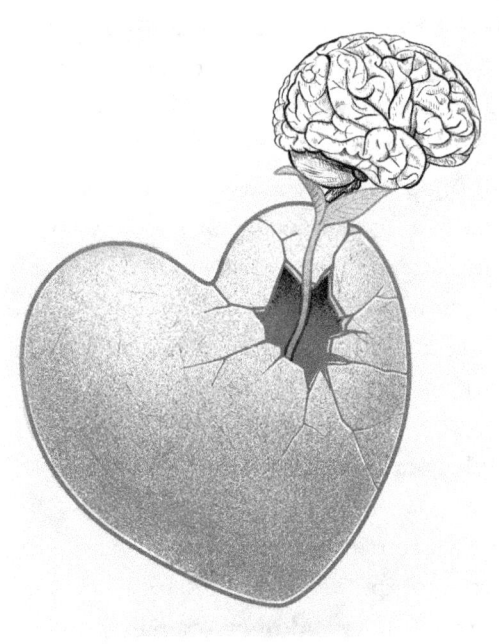

When we talk about workplaces, it's important to remember that they aren't just a place where we do work. Workplaces are also a place where we interact with other humans, many of whom walk around with unhealed pain patterns that can harm their colleagues. In order to be a stronger ally for your teammates and employees, as well as for your family and friends dealing with workplace trauma, it is important to understand how this type of trauma shows up in a person's life and to know how to support them.

## TYPICAL WAYS WORKPLACE TRAUMA SHOWS UP IN DAILY LIFE

### *The Sunday Blues (or Panic)*

Many people deal with a low-level of malaise on Sundays, but it tends to be worse in people with serious anxiety due to workplace trauma. It is common for people with abusive bosses or colleagues to exhibit extremely increased anxiety and/or depressive symptoms the day before they have to go back to work, whether that's a Sunday or a different day for an individual. One might think this is something predictable and easy to respond to with support, but that is far from guaranteed. For people who love their jobs, or who at least tolerate them without angst, it can be difficult to relate to and support someone stuck in a weekly cycle of stress, decompression, and then anxiety about the upcoming stress of the work week.

**Some examples of the Sunday Blues:**

- Mood shifts starting as early as two days before work will begin again for the week.
- Increased irritability and/or emotionality.

- Withdrawal: not wanting to do fun things, not wanting to engage, and being less verbal and/or less relational.
- Increased clinginess (the opposite of withdrawal) and wanting to have time/attention with safe people to distract from angst about work.
- Desire to talk about work a lot the day before, as well as attempts to predict what may or may not happen in the coming work week.
- Or the opposite, extreme resistance to talking about work. This can include anger outbursts related to any work-related topic.
- Increased aggression as a function of avoiding one's internal discomfort and deflecting it outward: slamming doors, picking fights, nagging people they live with, etc.
- In extreme situations or in homes where addiction is present, increased drinking/drug use or avoidance behaviors such as gambling.

These reactions can be common when someone is in a cycle of extreme anxiety around workplace trauma. It can be hard for some people to understand why the day-before-work blues are stronger in a person than their emotions during the middle of the work week. In some cases, a person in a toxic work environment is stressed and anxious all the time; others may be able to grin and bear it during the work week as a means of survival. This can resemble a fight-or-flight response that allows the person to just deal with a situation while they are in it, then panic about having to face it again; the next week, the cycle repeats.

Everyone is unique and each individual responds to their own work trauma based on many different factors, including a pre-history of trauma informing the current one. However, it is pretty typical that contemplating returning to a place or situation where abuse is present brings up fears and worries about everything that could go badly. These questions are usually related to potential workplace events that are unpredictable and how those events could impact them emotionally and mentally.

**Some recommendations for accommodations:**

- If this is a colleague, text or call them on Sundays (or the day before their work week begins) to check in and/or let them know you are there for them throughout the week.
- If this is someone you live with, either give them space or be available, depending on how they prefer to get support. Some people process by being alone, and others process by being with others.
- Help the person focus on the things in their environment they can control and minimize the focus on what they cannot.
- Provide fun distractions when appropriate: go for a hike, watch a funny movie, buy a new outfit, go for a spa day or massage.
- Be a consistent and supportive voice of reason. Validate that their situation is hard and support them in acknowledging that this is a difficult experience. Many people try to minimize other people's suffering to make themselves more comfortable, but this is not a helpful response to someone dealing with any sort of pain or trauma.

These accommodations may seem basic, but they go a long way in supporting a person coping with preemptive work-week blues, depression, and/or anxiety. So many people seek to distance themselves from those in their life who are suffering, for their own comfort, but this is truly the worst thing you can do when someone you care about is going through a hard time. Presence, acceptance, support, and consistency are key.

## WORKPLACE TRAUMA: THINGS TO LOOK OUT FOR

### *Periods of Irritability or Anger*

While irritability and anger are normal reactions to any kind of trauma, they can be particularly acute when dealing with ongoing workplace trauma. You may notice that your friend or loved one is more reactive during periods of high anxiety and, in general, it is not uncommon for people immersed in workplace trauma to take it out on those closest to them.

**Some examples of how irritability and anger show up in a person coping with workplace trauma:**

- Finding fault with little things that may seem mundane to another person.
- Mood swings that may be confusing to people around them and that can seem personal even though they are not.
- Heightened aggression on the road or with cashiers, in a way that wasn't typical for this person prior to being exposed to workplace trauma.
- Appearing more judgmental than prior to this experience, in a way that seems deflective, diminishing, or projecting.
- Quicker to pick fights or react poorly to a minor disagreement.
- Negative attitude about life or the world in general.
- Panic symptoms, such as increased heart rate, pacing, inability to sit still, or feeling frozen and immobile.

If you care about someone with workplace trauma, some of this irritability and aggression can be hurtful at times. The key here is to understand that it has nothing to do with you and to respond with kindness while setting boundaries for yourself. It is absolutely okay to let the person know if they are hurting you, and if they are overly critical of you in a way that seems heightened—

you don't have to just tolerate this behavior. But if you can recognize these behaviors can be a reflection of how they are feeling in a workplace that feels entrapping, it will help you avoid taking their behavior personally. A caged lion who feels there is no way out will absolutely attack. And as the saying goes, we always hurt the ones we love the most—this is absolutely true for people regularly reacting to their trauma wounds.

**Some recommended accommodations for the person experiencing irritation/aggression as a result of workplace trauma:**

- Show curiosity when they lash out. Ask questions: "Hey, are you having a hard time?" or "I know you are probably stressed about work tomorrow, is there anything I can do to support you?" or "I can tell you are having a hard day, is there anything you need?" These comments don't endorse their aggressive behavior, but they show compassion for the challenge this person faces without taking their aggression on as a personal attack.
- Be consistent in your reactions to your own emotions towards them (don't react to their reaction) and towards yourself (take a walk, go to a movie, call a friend of your own).
- Let them know that you notice they are picking on you a lot or are more aggressive than usual, and ask if something is on their mind that they need to talk about.
- Provide space, both for them and for you, when things are particularly intense.
- Allow them to apologize and take accountability for their actions, when appropriate. Don't minimize apologies by saying things like, "Oh, it is okay," or "No big deal."

**Some recommended accommodations for you as the loved one of a survivor:**

- Spend time with people who are in a healthier place emotionally and can also support you. When someone is in a really rough place, it isn't the time to expect support from them; it's better to go to other people for now who can provide that.
- Exercise regularly, enjoy a fun time with yourself or others, and eat well.
- Pursue hobbies or activities that make you feel good, such as artistic endeavors, projects, or community involvement.

It is really important to reiterate here that this person is suffering. It can sometimes be difficult to love someone who takes their pain out on you, but holding that space for them is a sign that you are one of the only people they feel safe with or can trust. Again, this doesn't mean tolerating unacceptable behavior. It just means being patient and asking yourself if, given the same set of circumstances, you might be responding to and/or feeling this pain in a similar way.

### *Feeling Frozen and/or Despairing About the Future*

When someone is in the throes of workplace trauma, it can feel paralyzing. Most of their weeks are threaded with anxiety and fear. They don't always know where to turn and can sometimes even feel hopeless. The person who is hurting may vacillate between obsessively looking for other jobs, to feeling like there is no safe place to turn and they are powerless to leave their current circumstance. This is a really hard consequence of workplace trauma, because someone with previously solid self-esteem can be undone by an untenable and/or abusive work situation. For people with a precarious sense of self-esteem at best, this experience can *really* drag them all the way down into feelings of hopelessness and despair.

**Some examples of how feeling frozen and despairing may show up after workplace traumas:**

- Showing signs of isolation and avoidance of social interactions, even with the people who make them feel joyful or good.
- Exhibiting an increased inability to see any of their own talents or skills.
- Refusal to see any of their positive qualities and/or cringing when another person tries to give them positive feedback.
- Forgetting a potentially substantial history of successes and filtering everything through the lens of their current challenges and perceived failure.
- Believing that they are no longer capable of anything at work or beyond. They translate feeling rejected, hurt, or unsafe at work into all other areas of their life.

**Some recommended accommodations:**

- If this is someone you have known for a long time, remind them of the many positive things you remember them achieving and give them specific examples.
- If this is a colleague, point out the ways in which this person makes your workplace a better place. Be specific with your compliments.

- If this is a person you haven't known for a really long time, ask them questions about their past and highlight the things they share that show success and their many amazing qualities.
- Do little things that show you care. Buy them coffee, bring them a treat, send or give them a card.

It is excruciatingly hard to live in a world where going to work is scary. Even though so many people want the person to just fix the problem or find another job, it is ridiculous to assume that these situations are that simple. Work stuff is complicated. It hits on the very thing we as humans need most outside of air, food, and water: to feel that we are financially and emotionally safe and secure. When someone's work life—and therefore, potentially their financial life—is in jeopardy, it is an utterly dismantling thing to experience.

Of course, the examples in this book are only a few of the ways that a person may react to workplace trauma, but they are a good place to start. As always, remember to care for yourself first before you attempt to help someone else. You are always better for others when you are best to yourself. And you will be an exponential support to your loved ones coping with workplace trauma if you are feeling good about and within yourself as well.

## CALL TO ACTION

Let's go back to your list. What about the overview of workplace trauma surprised you? Of what were you already aware? Is there anyone in your life at the moment who may be coping with such a thing? Is this something you have experienced and/or may even be experiencing now? Add any symptoms you see in those you know coping with workplace trauma that seem important. Tell those in your life who may be dealing with this that you want to be there for them and are doing your best to learn how to do that. Of course, if you are the affected person, try opening up to a friend or safe person about what you are dealing with and ask that they try to support you.

Spend some time thinking about if you have covered everything you wanted to so far regarding workplace trauma. You can always go back and reread and/or review anything in your list. This is tough stuff, and you are doing a great job simply being open to learning more and becoming more of an ally to yourself and others by increasing your Trauma Intelligence.

# CHAPTER 11

# COLLECTIVE/COMMUNAL TRAUMA AND HOW IT IMPACTS OUR LIVES

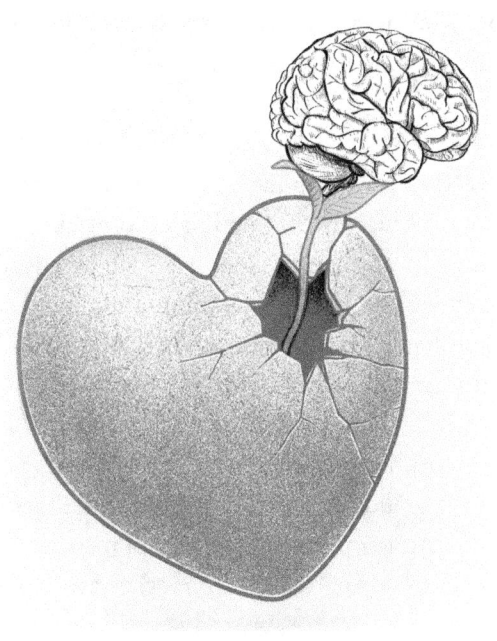

This is a unique time to be writing about collective and/or communal trauma, while the world is in the midst of the COVID-19 pandemic. Right now, every time we look at a phone, computer, or television we're met with a constant barrage of statistics and confusing opinions. Businesses have changed, millions of people are out of work or fear losing their jobs, hundreds of thousands of people have lost loved ones to this disease, and many people are terrified to leave their house even to go to the grocery store. In some ways, we are in a global experience that mirrors what so many people with anxiety and other mental health issues live with every day all year, and it's brought many of us to our knees.

What is different about this pandemic, as opposed to other types of trauma we have already covered, is that very few people on the planet are unaware of it. While COVID-19 has certainly impacted some countries and communities more than others, it is something that almost everyone is aware of and, therefore, impacted by. This is an unprecedented experience for most of us as individuals, but it is something that we are experiencing together.

That's where further explanation of collective trauma comes in. Collective trauma is unique in that it can both induce mass hysteria and panic, but also in that it isn't something a person usually experiences in a vacuum. Traumas such as childhood abuse, catastrophic events, or ambiguous trauma often make the person enduring them feel more different, more isolated, more ashamed, and more alone. Collective trauma creates a different type of experience, and in some cases can actually bring individuals and communities together in ways that other types of trauma cannot.

Right now I could pick up the phone and talk to ten or fifteen or twenty different people who will all tell me that the pandemic both scares and exhausts them, and that they are starting to notice unusual symptoms of depression and shutting down. That shared experience doesn't change the fact that those individuals are stressed and in emotional pain, but it does change the fact that they don't have to hide out and keep their feelings a secret. Simply because other people know about what is going on, they aren't necessarily coping with the pain all alone.

It is important to note that this doesn't mean people aren't feeling isolated as a by-product of this pandemic. However, it does mean that other people can relate in real-time to them feeling alone—that is the key difference here between collective trauma and other types. With other types of trauma, the real-time impact often leads to secrecy, shame, and differentiation. With communal trauma, there can be identification, collaboration, and in some cases, increased emotional community. That isn't to say that all communal trauma leads to increased community, but it is certainly more possible with collective trauma than with the other types discussed in this book.

■ ■ ■

Let's put aside the current state of the world and look at a different type of collective trauma. For example, what if an entire athletic team is killed at once in a plane crash? Such events have happened: think of the Humboldt Broncos bus crash in Canada in 2018, or the Yaroslavl Lokomotiv plane crash in Russia in 2011. This type of trauma could be classified as both catastrophic and communal. It is catastrophic in the sense that it is an unpredictable and horrifying event that comes out of nowhere. It is communal in that the entire community of parents, teachers, neighbors, and community members are enduring it all at the same time.

Does the communal nature of this loss lessen the individual tragedy for each person who lost a friend, family member, significant other, or neighbor in this event? Of course not. But it does allow them to come together in their pain in ways that make them feel less insane or confused or alone in this event.

None of this is to say that communal trauma is not terrible to experience. Nobody would or could argue that this pandemic is not devastating, or that losing an entire athletic team in a plane crash is not a tragedy. In fact, a catastrophic and communal loss such as the plane crash, can, and most likely will, forever change the entire community in which it happened. For weeks, months, years, and most likely decades after the incident, there will be grief, memorials, tears, and stories told about the incident. The school, families, and neighborhood involved will forever be touched by the loss—so much so that generations later, people who didn't know any of the members of the team will still talk about it as part of their shared history.

This community involvement and experience, even over multiple generations, allows the stories of those lost to live on in a way that can be simultaneously gut-wrenching and meaningful. It can give a sense of purpose to their loss, as opposed to a situation with one person who suffered alone and has a story that maybe one, max two, people—likely paid professionals—will ever know the details of.

Another notable aspect of collective trauma can be illustrated through our plane-crash example. In the community that experienced the plane crash tragedy, even local mental health professionals will be impacted and potentially even connected or related to the victims. This allows the people working with those mental health professionals to themselves feel more strongly connected with them, as they can share stories and memories in a way that a professional who is working with someone dealing with an individual trauma cannot.

Collective trauma, unlike most other types of trauma, may also lead to vital communal change. Dedications, services, plaques in people's honor, news articles, the list goes on—all of these are

## COLLECTIVE/COMMUNAL TRAUMA AND HOW IT IMPACTS OUR LIVES

often a part of collective loss and pain. There is a sense of celebration of those lost that really only lends itself to such experiences, though of course it comes after the initial shock and horrible grief have eased.

It's important to note that one's response to collective trauma is also dependent on their personal history of other types of trauma. This distinguishing factor is a very important nuance to consider when looking at group-impacted trauma and reactions to it. A person with a substantial history of trauma who has worked through a lot of it may, in some cases, have more tools to cope than someone with no previous trauma. On the other hand, a person with a lot of past traumatic experiences who hasn't worked through them may have a much more significant reaction to an already difficult situation of collective loss and trauma.

This distinction is a really important reminder that we do not all come to the same trauma from the same place. The healthier, more healed, and more resilient a person is, the more likely they will be to face, address, and cope with any other significant events in life, including a collective trauma experience.

■ ■ ■

Now let's look at a different type of collective trauma that spans generations, but doesn't necessarily involve a person's current experience—for example, the Holocaust or other systemic traumas that are centered on ethnicity or race and have impacted countless people? This type of ancestral trauma does filter down through the shared stories and collective experiences of those who are born in these communities. But it also continues to reverberate in harmful ways that, unlike the other types of collective trauma already discussed, do not necessarily lead to eventual celebration of the victims, but do include ongoing loss, unfair consequence, and pain.

We need not look far to see the continued reverberations of racism in our current world—it is present in every aspect of modern life, from the penal system to the education system to the housing system. For anyone to assert that the experience of racism has not, in current times, continued as an ongoing form of collective trauma would be delusional. While this type of communal trauma does allow for some relational experiences among those who have endured it, it also creates a secondary ambiguous trauma that is always present—a continuous reality of the vestiges of that original (and ongoing) wound.

In any sort of work towards Trauma Intelligence, these distinctions between collective trauma must be considered. Collective trauma that can also include ongoing, ambiguous trauma that is not only relevant, but impactful, is crucial to understand. Finally, it is important to always remember that collective trauma is not only a larger category under which catastrophic trauma lies, but also one that induces heightened pain from previously experienced and yet unhealed childhood trauma.

CHAPTER 12

# COLLECTIVE/COMMUNAL TRAUMA: THINGS TO LOOK OUT FOR

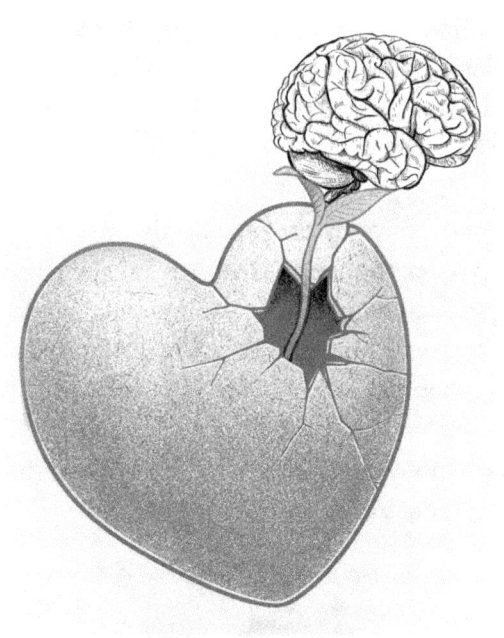

As already discussed, collective trauma is an experience that happens within a group of people who can all relate to a shared experience. That experience can create several kinds of trauma reactions and echoing results; at the same time, and in other ways, it can sometimes bring people more closely together.

Let's look at 12-step recovery programs, for example. These groups include people, most of whom have experienced many types of trauma, who have found their lives to be so painful that they must find a new way to cope. Each individual in the group has a unique history and story, but they can all relate to a common experience like drug addiction or alcoholism. You cannot enter the room of a 12-step recovery meeting without feeling both sadness and levity at the same time. Shared inside jokes, slogans, and commentaries bring this group of people, who may have many differences between them, together in a way that produces both value and meaning.

The trauma experienced by the individuals in this group of people was not collective or simultaneous, but the healing of their specific traumas happens in a communal way. Therefore, the shared pain experience has brought people together rather than split them apart.

The more cohesive nature of collective trauma, while helpful in a lot of ways, does not mean that there are not painful outcomes that result. In fact, some of the most jarring effects of communal trauma can be so intense that they change the fabric of how a society or group of people perceive, respond to, and engage in the world.

Let's look more closely at are some key ways that communal trauma can and does impact a person's life.

# TYPICAL WAYS COLLECTIVE TRAUMA SHOWS UP IN DAILY LIFE

## *Heightened Sense of Panic and/or Loss of Faith*

One of the key ways that communal or collective trauma impacts a person is by fundamentally changing their worldview. A person who once was trusting and calm might become overy alert or assume another potential tragedy is always just around the corner. This can lead to a worst-case-scenario mentality that harms not just that individual but also the people with whom they interact. A major factor in coping with communal traumas such as bombings, pandemics, or planes crashing into the Twin Towers—is that the world no longer feels normal or as it once was, thus; a shift in anxiety, depression, and/or world engagement can be the result.

**Some examples of how heightened sense of panic and/or loss of faith in the world at large show up:**

- Dramatic increases in the symptoms of depression and anxiety: for example, sleeping too much or not sleeping at all, gaining weight or not being able to eat at all.
- Increased negative commentary and focus on things in the world that are not safe or working, as opposed to a focus on those that are.
- Anticipatory anxiety around things, such as trying to predict the next significant world event, accident, or disaster ahead of time so as not to be blindsided again.
- Less goal setting and dreaming about the future and increased pragmatism.

- Watching more news and or heightened/stressful television content and/or talking a lot more than usual about world events. This comes both from a desire to stay informed and a desire to be prepared in case something else is coming that could potentially be harmful.
- Withdrawal from activities that once brought joy, such as exercise, travel, cooking, or talking with friends,.
- Periods of panic and feeling stuck, in ways that were previously uncommon and/or less intense.

This is certainly not an exhaustive list; however, these reactions are very common after an experience of collective trauma. While you may also be experiencing the same collective trauma as someone else who is struggling, that doesn't mean you can't be more attuned to how to support those you care about during a hard time.

**Some recommendations for accommodations:**

- Be willing to listen to the person's fears about the future and, instead of providing aggressive suggestions or insisting they remain positive, validate their fears in a supportive and reasonable way.
- Make recommendations for shared experiences that can bring joy, such as cooking together, watching something comical together, going for a long walk, or just having a video chat if you haven't seen one another in a while.
- Encourage them to keep their space clean, and to even beautify it in some way that allows for increased creativity and care. For example, they can add plants they can care for, paint a wall to invoke more inspiration, or clean a closet and make it super organized.

- Point out positive things you see in the world—if the person is in a space to hear about it, and focus, when appropriate, on topics that can induce hope more than fear.
- Remind the person of their strengths and successes, especially if you notice their self-esteem is lagging or that they are forgetting all the positive things they experienced in life prior to this trauma.

These accommodations are straightforward, but they go a long distance when trying to help someone in the throes of a collective trauma reaction feel supported. The nice thing about these ideas is that they can foster connection as well as hope. You can also direct these accommodations towards yourself, if you are the one currently coping with reactions to collective trauma.

### *Increased Reactions to Previous Trauma*

While some people experiencing communal trauma have no substantial prior trauma history, many do. In that case, experiences like feeling trapped from a pandemic or overwhelmed by anxiety because of a bombing can also trigger vestigial pain related to feeling trapped due to childhood sexual abuse or overwhelmed by loud noises of screaming or hitting or slamming things in a violent childhood home. When one's central nervous system is already compromised due to historical trauma, a collectively traumatic experience can heighten those responses for a period of time.

**Some examples of how increased reactions to previous trauma show up in a person who has experienced collective trauma:**

- Increased startle response.
- Increased symptoms of mild paranoia, such as fear of being trapped or fear of being hit or harmed in some way, when there is no immediate threat.

- Vulnerability to resume or increase addictive behaviors that had either ceased or greatly diminished prior to the collective trauma.
- More pronounced emotional swings, from anger to despair to terror to extreme anxiety to dissociation.
- More substantial neediness of those around them, including wanting more time to talk and process things that they are dealing with.
- Conversely, decreased relational contact and diminished sociability or support seeking, which can lead to dangerous levels of isolation.

If you care about someone who is not only experiencing communal trauma but also has a history of other trauma that is reactivated as a result, there are some simple accommodations you can offer to help them through this difficult time.

**Some recommended accommodations for the survivor:**

- Help them remember the choices they have now in their lives, as opposed to the more limited choices they had as a child stuck in a home they could not leave.
- Care for yourself appropriately, so you have more emotional reserves to offer when they do have an increased need for support and connection.
- Allow them to process their feelings without trying to fix where they are, but also do not endorse behaviors such as extreme isolation and withdrawal.
- Remind them they are not alone, that you care, and that you notice their symptoms, while also asking them how you can best support them during this time.

## COLLECTIVE/COMMUNAL TRAUMA: THINGS TO LOOK OUT FOR

- In situations of severe isolation, simply show up at their house with food and let them know you are there to help. When someone is in extreme isolation mode, it begets a desire for more isolation. In these cases, showing up may be helpful. Make sure, however, you have the level of closeness in the relationship where this makes sense and feels safe to them, so as not to surprise them or make them feel trapped in another way.

This can be a really hard time for you to show support to a person who is experiencing multiple layers of trauma reactions at the same time. If you are also struggling, don't give more than you have—you always have to take care of yourself first. If you notice the person has increased troubling symptoms like self-harm, morose speaking or thinking, or heightened physical symptoms, it is crucial that you recommend they get serious professional help. In these situations, it is paramount to remember you can support another person, but you cannot save them.

### *Wanting to Make Extreme or Sudden Changes*

One of the repercussions of collective trauma is a fear of loss of control. When massive events happen, it not only impacts one's sense of survival and safety, but it also makes the person experiencing it realize they likely had zero control over this event happening and could not have prevented it. When this instinct of attempted control over life gets threatened, it can incite a person to find extreme ways to create another illusion of control. Sometimes change is a positive thing; however, if someone you know is talking about an extreme change with very little forethought either during or right after experiencing a collective trauma, that may be a warning sign.

**Some examples of how the desire to make extreme or sudden changes can show up:**

- Talking about selling everything and moving across the country.
- Wanting to end a long-term relationship, seemingly out of nowhere.
- Making extreme statements that can appear as all or nothing in context.
- Increased symptoms of mania, euphoria, and/or risk-taking.
- Wanting to lash out at and/or seek revenge on someone due to mild frustrations.
- Talking about out-of-nowhere job changes, life changes, or relationship changes that seem counter to what you have known about this person.

**Some recommended accommodations:**

- Validate the feeling, not the story.
- Encourage them to make decisions only after things calm down, or after they have ensured this is not a decision from which they cannot return.
- Offer to make a pros and cons list.
- Ask follow-up questions that can support the person in considering how they came to this decision.
- If you are close enough, directly state that perhaps they are feeling a fear of loss of control. Ask if, given another set of circumstances, this choice would make sense.
- Remind the person that they can still make this choice a few months down the road if they decide to hold out for now.

It is traumatizing to experience something that causes us to recognize that the majority of life and the world are out of control.

## COLLECTIVE/COMMUNAL TRAUMA: THINGS TO LOOK OUT FOR

It exhausts all of our resources for feeling empowered and goal driven. It makes us feel small and vulnerable and, in some cases, wholly terrified.

In some situations, it is totally appropriate—and even favorable—to make a massive life change. The key here is to digest where that desire for change is coming from, and then to respond accordingly. Is the desire for extreme change coming from a spiritual or personal awakening of sorts, one about what matters and how one wants to spend one's time given the finite nature of life? Or is it coming from an intense fear of loss of control—a desire to run and escape and avoid all the pain of the experience? That question is integral in these situations, and is one that will be helpful for you to bring up to your friend or loved one who is dealing with the desire for extreme change after a collective trauma.

## CALL TO ACTION

Take out that list. How are you feeling about the list so far? Are you surprised at how many traumas you have highlighted? Conversely, are there fewer than you anticipated? Add in any experiences you may have had with collective trauma that you previously had not recognized. How about symptoms that you or someone you love have exhibited that, until now, you had not considered? As always, tell the people in your life coping with such issues that you are there for them; also, ask those same people if they can look out for you in these ways as well.

So often, we want to help but don't know *how*. Be specific with others about what you need and how they can help—and also what you can offer and how you can help. This can go a long way in creating meaningful connections during a very difficult time.

Take some time to process all you have read about collective trauma, and what that means for you and your loved ones. Rereading is always an option, if you need more time with the material. Collective trauma is a far more textured and nuanced experience than we could possibly cover in a few chapters. However, just by taking the time to learn what you have so far, you are way ahead of the curve.

# CHAPTER 13

# OTHER TYPES OF TRAUMA TO CONSIDER

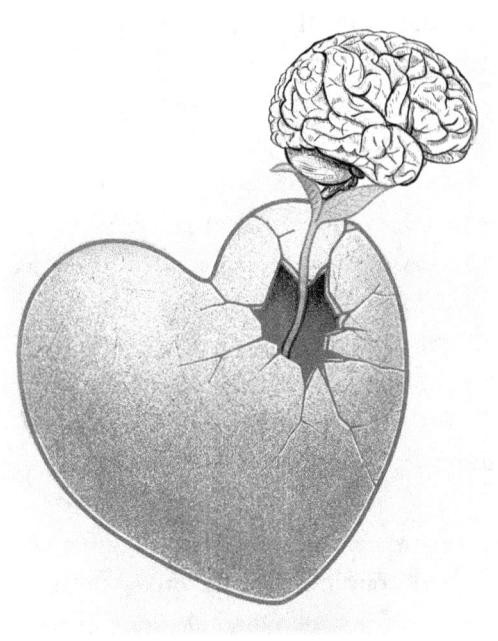

So far, we have reviewed five primary categories of trauma. While those categories cover a wide breadth of trauma-related experiences, they do not in any way cover them all. Focusing on increasing one's Trauma Intelligence and ability to understand, process, and respond effectively to varying traumas includes an awareness of as many types and variations of trauma as possible. For that reason, I will provide a shorter overview of five other categories of trauma to consider and learn about going forward.

## MEDICAL TRAUMA

**Medical trauma is any trauma related to a medical diagnosis, experience, or process. More specifically, medical traumas can include, but are not limited to:**

- Surgical trauma related to waking up during surgery, having the wrong surgery or operation due to medical negligence, injury, or other damage as a result of surgery for a primary condition. Surgical trauma can also include having anxiety before, during, and/or after a surgical procedure.
- Long-term presenting medical concerns or symptoms that go misdiagnosed over a long period of time, leading to feelings of isolation, confusion, and fear along with, potentially, increased symptomatology.
- Chronic pain or illness related to medical conditions, including back pain, immune illnesses, cancer, heart disease, diabetes, and/or any number of diagnoses that cause long-term pain.
- Medical treatment trauma, which occurs when treatment for a medical condition causes other chronic pain or secondary illness. This can include long-term radiation and chemotherapy, heart medication causing a chronic kidney

condition, or steroids causing weight gain and chronic pain. One paramount issue is that when a strong medical treatment is required for an otherwise life-threatening illness, there can be many secondary side effects and illnesses as a result. This puts the patient in a situation where, in order to save one's life, one must make the decision to accrue increased symptoms and pain.

- Trauma related to a life-threatening illness or the fear of death.
- Medical trauma-related to a diagnosis that is initially terminal, and then becomes non-terminal. This may sound strange as a source of trauma; however, the experience puts the person at high alert for the condition's return and a potential future terminal diagnosis.
- Trauma related to the loss of social engagement, financial security, and relational support due to a chronic or acute medical condition.
- Medical trauma from the loss of predictability in life or a feeling of being in control of one's medical choices and/or health.

While each of these types of medical trauma could be elaborated on in great detail, I'd like to share an anecdote for one of them. This story may seem confusing, but it's a common and important type of medical trauma to understand.

Many years ago, I headed up admissions for a graduate school of social work. One of the things I loved most about that job was getting to know and engaging with nontraditional students.

One of my favorite students ever was in her mid-60s when she applied and earned a scholarship to the program. She was so eager to begin that I was taken completely by surprise when she phoned to let me know that her husband had been unexpectedly diagnosed with a terminal brain tumor and had been given a maximum of two months to live. As one may imagine, the hopeful student was traumatized and asked to put her admission on hold. Of course, I obliged.

At this point, you may think you can predict how this story will go. I can assure you, you may be just as surprised at the outcome as I was.

A few weeks into the diagnosis, she and her husband came to the university to see me—and they reported a bizarre turn of events. According to her husband's follow-up MRI, the terminal tumor appeared to be completely and totally gone. In this situation, it was hard to know if the first MRI was just wrong, or if this situation was what the doctors alleged—that sometimes terminal tumors disappear. If that happens, the patient knows that the tumor will one day return.

Given this information, you might also think you know how this couple would respond. You might even consider this situation some sort of miracle. However, upon talking to our potential student's husband, I could see he was in acute distress about this news.

I talked to him at length. He shared that he had already prepared himself to die from this tumor—and that, because of what the doctors had told him about its eventual return, he found it impossible to feel hopeful. This made him feel more confused and out of control, like he had to keep one eye open at all times, waiting for this thing to come back. Even if the doctors were wrong and read the incorrect MRI, that didn't take away the fact that he couldn't know for sure—and couldn't trust that he was healthy and well.

I share this story because it taught me a valuable lesson about medical trauma. Sometimes what seems like hopeful news to one person is terrifying and challenging information for another. It also taught me that there are so many nuances to medical experiences and the life and death cycle. Therefore, we should always listen to the person experiencing a situation, not to what we presume we would feel or do in their place.

If there is one piece of feedback to offer here in terms of developing your Trauma Intelligence related to people with medical challenges: always hear what they have to say and never, ever assume you know what you would feel or do if you haven't been in that situation yourself. Even if you *have* been in a similar situation, don't assume the person feels or will react the same way you did.

If you can offer someone that small bit of support, you will be leaps and bounds ahead of everyone else.

## RELATIONAL TRAUMA

One type of trauma that is particularly nuanced and potentially confusing is relational trauma. This type of trauma results from any relationship with or adjacent to someone that causes an adverse impact on the affected person's life. Relational trauma can be related to anything from someone who is physically violent, to someone who gaslights, to someone who appears to be one way and then proves to be another. It is not only part of the objective reality of living life while engaging with other human beings—relational trauma is also a subjective and very textured and personal experience for the person going through it.

**Relational trauma can include, but is not limited to:**

- Any relationship with a person who starts off as supportive and overly engaged, and ends up behaving in confusing ways that are counter to who they initially presented themselves to be.
- Trauma related to physical, emotional, mental, religious, intellectual, and/or sexual violence in adulthood that can both mirror childhood trauma and ignite trauma not previously present.

- Unsafe relationships that take over a person's safety and life, such as an abusive neighbor, a stalker, a person who will not respect clearly set boundaries, or an abusive or toxic person.
- Trauma related to feeling trapped, with no financial or escape options, with an abusive partner or person.
- Trauma related to lack of trust in anyone due to previous childhood or relational trauma, which has contributed to a diminished sense of safety in the world around the person.
- Being left as the result of one's own unresolved trauma or hurtful behaviors.

As you can see from the examples, relational trauma can be a type of trauma that starts with childhood abuse, then lends a person to finding repeated traumatic situations that mirror familiar experiences. But it can also be a type of trauma that comes out of nowhere through a negative experience in or near a relationship with another person.

The experience of being stalked is a type of relational trauma that is often under discussed. If you or anyone you know has ever had a stalker, you know that this can make a person feel terrified and unstable in almost every area of their life. Relentless stalking can be truly horrifying to experience; in some situations, a stalker will go to any length possible to engage with, find, assert control over, and/or terrorize their target. I've known and worked with people who had stalkers follow them to different jobs, towns, shopping venues, and homes. Without specific and detailed proof that this person is following them, it can be difficult to press charges and/or find a solution. In fact, some stalkers are very good at manipulation and can convince police authorities that they are the ones being stalked, not their victims.

While this type of relational trauma is somewhat rare, it's important to remember that it can be life altering when it does happen. Stalking leads the victim to feelings of paranoia, anxiety, and a total fear of connection. If you know someone who has experienced or is experiencing stalking, it is crucial that you listen to them and support them in any way possible. At the same time, it is also important that you protect your own identity and safety, keeping social media use in mind in particular, while you support the affected person.

Supporting a friend or loved one who is being stalked can be particularly difficult, as sometimes stalkers try to find and engage with those closest to their primary subject of focus. It is crucial to be a listening ear to the person who is being stalked, while also maintaining a sense of distance on social media and other online outlets where you could potentially be tracked to this person. With this type of trauma, assisting your loved one or friend in finding safe and sound legal counsel and a really seasoned mental health professional are particularly useful.

## FINANCIAL TRAUMA

Another type of trauma that often goes undiscussed is financial trauma. As with relational trauma, financial trauma is nuanced—in addition to being a stand-alone trauma, it can also fall in a subcategory with other types.

**For example, financial trauma can be related to varying circumstances that can include, but are not limited to:**

- Being in a relationship where there is financial control by one party that limits the other party's escape options.
- Unexpected lawsuits or investment catastrophes, or expenses that seem insurmountable to catch up on. This can include medical bills, legal fees, divorce costs, and estate expenses, among other things.

- Sudden loss of a job, without the ability to receive unemployment or another sufficient stream of income.
- Loss of one's entire life savings through illegal investment scams (think Bernie Madoff) or economic catastrophes.
- Theft of one's money through situations including abusive relationships, financial scams, or robbery.
- Loss of one's entire home due to a natural disaster, which can also lead to secondary financial loss and trauma.
- Systemic and generational poverty that feels insurmountable to move beyond.
- Growing up with financial insecurity, which can include not knowing when your next meal is coming, or if there will be water or electricity when you get home from school. This can also be rooted in childhood trauma.

As you can see from the list above, financial trauma can start as early as childhood, and can even span back through generations of family members. But it can also be sudden and unexpected. A person who has money at any one given time will not necessarily always have money. Systemic poverty is one of the harshest and most ongoing ambiguous traumas a person can endure. It is also troubling to suffer the consequences of one's own poor financial choices—some of which may have been learned in childhood and must be addressed to be healed.

Another aspect of financial trauma is loss through theft or deceit. Take the Bernie Madoff Ponzi scheme. This person single-handedly manipulated, hoodwinked, and stole millions of dollars from many people. And he didn't just steal—he did it with a smile and a promise of trustworthiness. People who invested with Madoff literally ended up with nothing left to show for an entire lifetime of savings. Some even completed suicide as a result. While one may argue that people with money can always make more money, that does not negate the fact that people spent decades of their lives building something, only to have it taken from them without warning amid a breach of trust.

Another type of financial trauma mentioned above is financial control by a parent or significant other, where the person being controlled cannot find any way to escape their unsafe and untenable living situation. This can also fall under other types of trauma, including relational trauma, but it is definitely worth noting as a separate experience. This sort of financial trauma leads to feelings of fear, a lack of safety, and insecurity about one's ability to care for oneself financially.

Supporting people you care about who are enduring financial trauma can be challenging. While it isn't your job to rescue anyone financially, there are other things you can do to be helpful. You can listen. You can let the person share about their fear and anxiety related to their financial crisis. You can show total non-judgment and not force the person into some toxically positive narrative about a situation that, for them, feels truly tragic. You can also offer supportive suggestions, recommendations and referrals as is appropriate.

Many people disappear when others have trauma, in general; however financial trauma is particularly tricky for some. As with all the other supportive recommendations in this book—just being there and doing so consistently (while of course always taking care of your own needs first), will go a long way in making a person who is coping with financial trauma feel seen, supported, cared for and heard.

## CYBER TRAUMA

Cyber trauma is a relatively new type of trauma, but an integral one to consider nonetheless. Under the umbrella of cyber trauma, there are many different ways that a person can experience and be subjected to challenging and potentially life-changing personal circumstances.

**Types of cyber trauma include, but are not limited to:**

- Cyberbullying, which is in some ways more relentless than in-person bullying. Nowadays, a person can bully someone at all times of the day and night if they have access to any technological device. This type of trauma can lead to remarkably decreased self-esteem and, in some situations, even suicide.
- Cyberstalking. This type of cyber trauma would also be included under relational trauma. Virtual stalking is another way that a person can be stalked, leading them to feel wholly unsafe in the world.
- Identity theft through cyber means, which can lead to financial loss and fear.
- Catfishing, which is a form of manipulation via dating platforms. In this situation, a person presents themselves to be someone else entirely, either real or fictional. This can cause confusion and even financial loss for the victim of this experience.

What happens when someone is being cyberbullied and goes through all the appropriate channels to end it: telling a safe person, blocking the bully on all devices, even reporting them to social media outlets? Sometimes it stops. Many other times, especially if the bully is relentless, they will create fake profiles and send abusive or incriminating messages in varying ways. This creates a situation where the person feels that they literally cannot escape the bully. This can make the recipient of this type of bullying start to feel paranoid in other aspects of their life as well.

The thing that further complicates cyberbullying is that if a person wants to engage in any reasonable way in our current world, they cannot be without some sort of technical device. Bullying that stays within the four walls of a school or office can have serious long-term impacts on its victims, but it also ends at some point during the day. But cyberbullying can extend to all social media outlets, emails, texts, calls—the list goes on. If numbers and accounts are blocked up, the bully can pop up again through a new one. As we have already established, that feeling of being unable to escape the source of one's discomfort can have a very severe impact on a person's life.

Validating the person who is being traumatized virtually can take several forms. First, you can offer, as always, a supportive ear. If you say you are available any time for them to call, then try to keep your promise when they do pick up the phone to reach out. If you have the ability or means to help them advocate with authority figures, community figures, social media outlets or other friends, doing so would also be very helpful. The reason advocacy can be so critical in supporting someone who is experiencing cyber trauma is because their self-esteem can be markedly decreased if they have been bombarded with constant negative messages online.

Reality testing is also a helpful thing to use and offer in support of a loved one or friend who has endured cyber trauma. Having them make lists of what is true and not true, in case the bullying has truly made them lose site of their sense of self and safety in the world; and helping them continue to connect to other supportive and reliable people in *real* life can both go a long way in making the person feel safer and more trusting again.

## CAREGIVER TRAUMA

When a person finds themselves in the position of being a caregiver for someone who is physically or mentally ill, it can be excruciatingly painful and difficult. In many cases, caregiver trauma is the result of being put in the often unexpected position of becoming emotionally, mentally, physically, and/or financially responsible for someone who would not otherwise be okay on their own. Part of the nature of caregiver trauma is the pain of seeing someone you love suffer; the other part of it is guilt, anger, fear, exhaustion, and feeling trapped.

**Caregiver trauma can include, but is not limited to:**

- Taking care of an adult child who is mentally or physically not able to care for themselves.
- Having a spouse, sibling, or friend who is chronically or terminally ill.
- Caring for an aging or ill parent.
- Feeling financially responsible for someone who cannot work independently.
- Ongoing trauma due to caring for anyone who is dependent for any or all their potential needs. This can fall as a subtype to ambiguous trauma.

If you or someone you know has ever been a caregiver, then you have either experienced or witnessed the extreme exhaustion and isolation that can occur as a result. Let's look at someone who has had a loved one living with life-threatening cancer. While the loved one may be enduring substantial medical trauma, their primary support or caregiver may be experiencing intense loneliness, anxiety, depression and fear related to both the constant needs they are being required to fill in the home, as well as the sadness around watching someone they deeply care about suffering.

While, of course, we would all like to consider ourselves to be the type of human being who would valiantly support and take care of our most trusted loved ones when they are ill; this does not mean we would not become overwhelmed, exhausted, angry and even completely flatlined as a result. To add to the challenges that a caregiver faces, there is often intense guilt when they are not with or looking out for or taking care of the person whom they are responsible for helping. This guilt then fuels more anxiety and overwhelm, because it leaves the person feeling as though they can't get any time for themselves.

In addition to caregiver trauma being something a person can experience in the home, this type of trauma can also happen to frontline medical professionals and caregivers who are with patients in their most trying of medical crises. Year after year and decade after decading of taking care of other people can lead to extreme burnout and even some mental health challenges.

As hard as it sounds to a person who is a primary caregiver of someone to consider, it is really important that you, as a supportive person in their life, encourage them to find at least a tiny bit of down time. You can offer to assist them occasionally in their caregiver duties, if that feels like the right choice for you and your needs. You can also help them find supportive organizations or services that can assist, depending on their financial status and needs, as a result. Additionally, you can cook for them, buy them an in-home massage (if touch is okay for them), offer to clean or hire someone to clean for them, and even help them find someone to take care of their lawn or their garden if that is getting out of hand.

In addition to offering practical and helpful support, you can absolutely call, check in, and listen. When someone is a caregiver to another person for years on end, most of their friends and acquaintances get tired of listening and disappear. This withdrawal then creates a secondary trauma and relational loss for the person.

It is very important to remember that just because you aren't the one who is in a caregiver role now, it doesn't mean this situation could not, at another time, absolutely happen to you. To that end, it is crucial that we all remember to lift those around us up when we are on an upswing in life. You will be a stand-out friend and support if you simply continue to show up for the caregiver, consistently over a long period of time.

## OTHER TYPES OF TRAUMA NOT YET IDENTIFIED

Throughout the course of this book, we have identified five main categories of trauma and five other categories of trauma. These categories each contain subtypes of trauma—and, to further complicate things, some of these traumas can fit into more than one of these categories at a time. Because trauma is simultaneously both objective and subjective, it is important to remember that no one book can include every single possible type of trauma that one can endure. For this reason, it is always important to remember that our level of Trauma Intelligence constantly needs to be addressed. We should all be consciously vigilant in learning about, trying to understand, and responding to trauma in empathic and impactful ways.

## CALL TO ACTION

Now it is time to take what you have learned thus far in this book and apply it to what you already know about trauma that, until now, you have not written about. Consider all the information about the trauma you have explored in the last several exercises. What other types of trauma come to mind that you feel have not yet been addressed here? How do these types of trauma experiences impact either you or someone you know? What tools and accommodations can you take from the previous chapters to apply to these other traumas that came up for you? What other accommodations would you like to add?

## SET SOME GOALS

Take some time to reflect on three action steps you would like to take going forward to ensure your continued education and growth toward Trauma Intelligence—and if necessary, to continue to nurture yourself in your own recovery. It is okay to keep this list of goals to yourself, but in some cases, it can be beneficial to share it with a trustworthy person. Spend some time thinking about how you want to hold yourself accountable for continuing on the path of more empathically, effectively, and compassionately responding to both your own trauma and that of the people you love.

# CHAPTER 14

# HOPE FOR HUMANITY

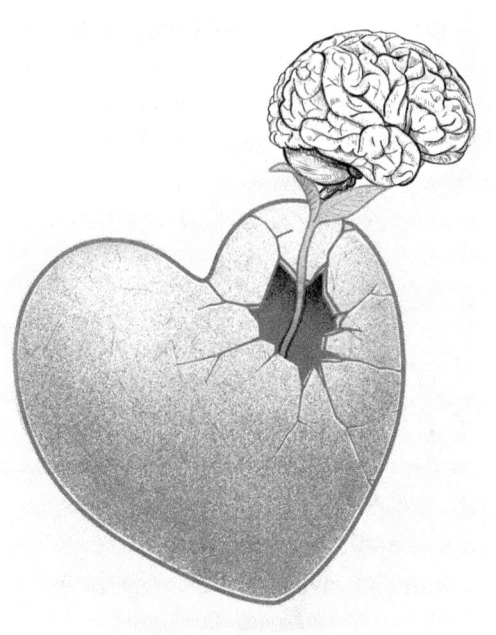

Some of the information in this book is hard to read. But it has certainly been far more difficult to live, if you have endured any of these trauma experiences. One thing that is often under-discussed in any exploration of trauma work or Trauma Intelligence building is that there is always the potential for hope on the other side of pain.

Even if our trauma or our hurts are sometimes unspeakable it doesn't mean that we cannot, bit by bit, work toward a process of personal healing and evolution. Just as the world is full of pain, it is also full of safe and wonderful human beings who would love the opportunity to learn and make a difference.

And if *you* are the person who cares, there is always an opportunity to make marked progress—and even recovery—in how we live with and respond to trauma in ourselves and those around us.

Some of the most incredible people I know who have made remarkable recoveries in living with the effects of their trauma experiences are my clients. Many people misconstrue the work I do; they assume that everything I hear and deal with must be sad and disappointing. While there is certainly an element of grief and a diminished sense of trust in the world that a professional working in trauma experiences, there is also the opportunity to facilitate and witness the dramatic transformation and healing a person is capable of accomplishing.

For this reason, it is important that you don't take what you have read in this book and use it to assume the world is filled with badness. Rather, assume that from pain, there is always the choice to walk the road toward growth, which comes in different ways for different people.

While some people take the path of traditional therapy to heal—and I would always recommend a highly seasoned and well-boundaried mental health professional for severe trauma experience recovery—others seek spirituality, educational endeavors, or even, as you are doing in taking the time to read this book, personal study and exploration.

There is no wrong way to heal or to change. The only action that will yield no change at all is total *inaction*. However seemingly small, any move to change yourself or to be a more supportive vessel of compassion toward others is impactful. And any intent to be of more service to ourselves and the people around us who are suffering is worthy of acknowledgment.

I also want to invite you to recognize that just the action of your reading this book, taking the time to do these exercises, and having even a modicum of interest in understanding and responding to trauma more effectively, is a very good sign about the state of the world in which we live. It is a sign of hope.

Most people don't come onto this planet with the desire to hurt others. Additionally, most people don't expect that any sort of external trauma, through catastrophe or illness or any number of other unpredictable life experiences, will ever happen to them. However, as anyone who has lived in the world knows, no matter how much control we try to assert over life, there is no way to predict when true love will find us. Equally true is that there is no way to predict when tragedy or pain will befall us either.

The best we can hope for in life is to be able to respond to both great love and great pain with compassion, patience, grace, personal accountability, and forgiveness. If we can all strive daily to attempt this sort of practice, in whatever ways make sense to us and feel most beneficial, then we can hope that life for everyone around us will be at least a little bit better for knowing us. At the very least, we won't be walking around inflicting more and more pain on a society that is already exponentially damaged.

> ## CALL TO ACTION
>
> List the five most painful experiences you have endured in your life so far. List the five most amazing experiences you can recall in your life up until today. How did those painful experiences inform who you are? How did the amazing ones impact you? What surprised you about each list? How can you take those experiences and integrate them into an action plan of hope, both for yourself and for those around you whom you care about and connect to the most?

## TRAUMA INTELLIGENCE IN YOUR DAILY LIFE

Everything you have learned here is an intellectual exercise in educating yourself and understanding trauma, Trauma Intelligence, and how it relates to you and the world around you. As with any good educational exercise, however, the most important part of this book will be the critical thinking you use to determine what you do and don't relate to—and how to integrate these bits of knowledge into an action plan of living that makes the most sense for your life, your personality, and the way that you perceive the world.

There is no wrong way to take this information, other than not to take it at all. And there is not only one path to exploring how this book can make the most impact within you and with the people in your world.

Over the coming days and weeks, I recommend that you continue the journaling exercises presented to you. Also, continue to review what you have read and consider how you can most effectively implement these ideas in your daily life.

When it comes to trying to integrate new ideas and practices, it is always best to start small and expand from there. Even tiny tweaks in behavior—such as asking your colleague how they are dealing with their recent divorce or saying hello to the neighbor who seems to be totally isolated and has no friends—can move mountains in the emotional worlds of people who are in pain.

What if *you* are the one who is in pain? What can you do in your life to allow more people in? To let someone be close to you who you keep trying to push away? To practice beginning to know that you are, in fact, worthy and you do, in fact, deserve to feel better about the world around you?

If you are here. If you are trying. If you are listening. If you desire to evolve—then you are already well on your way to developing a keener sense of trauma and an empathetic evolution toward true Trauma Intelligence. And as you go forward on your journey toward seeing and being compassionate in a world filled with pain, please take these three mantras with you:

- It is okay to ask for help.
- It is okay to offer help.
- It is absolutely okay to do both of those things imperfectly.

CHAPTER 15

# A SECOND BREAK IN CONSCIOUSNESS

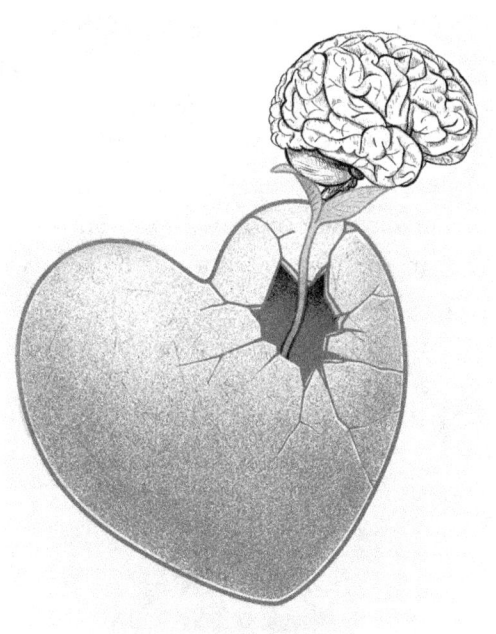

The inspiration to write this book began with the death of my sister. It ended with the death of one of my best friends.

On May 13, 2021, my friend Glendy died after a long battle with cancer. Unlike my sister's death, which was immediate and sudden, my friend fought beyond the comprehension of human capacity.

What I have found in these two recent losses is this: It doesn't matter how we die, as, at the end, there is always finality. Regardless of the way in which we depart, we are still missed and the legacy of who we are reverberates loudly.

In seeking to work on your own understanding of trauma and develop your own increased capacity for Trauma Intelligence, you are absolutely impacting this planet while you are still alive. In doing so, you are not only acknowledging the pain of those who are gone that may never have had the opportunity to heal fully, but you are also finding real and meaningful ways to make a difference while your time on Earth is still available to you.

My sister mattered. My friend mattered. You matter. Your life matters. Your story matters. The way in which you go about engaging in the world absolutely matters too.

None of the stories or experiences shared in this book are intended to make you sad. They are, however, intended to make you think. It is in the thinking and in the conscious reflection of your role in helping others that your life can begin to take on a purpose even stronger than that which you may have once considered.

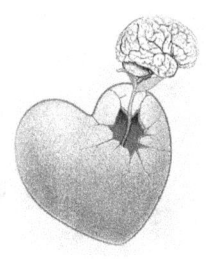

# BIBLIOGRAPHY

Francis, Darlene, Josie Diorio, Dong Liu, and Michael J. Meaney. "Nongenomic Transmission across Generations of Maternal Behavior and Stress Responses in the Rat." *Science* 286, no. 5442 (November 5, 1999): 1155–58. https://doi.org/10.1126/science.286.5442.1155.

Pfefferbaum, Betty, Elana Newman, Summer D. Nelson, Pascal Nitiéma, Rose L. Pfefferbaum, and Ambreen Rahman. "Disaster Media Coverage and Psychological Outcomes: Descriptive Findings in the Extant Research." *Current Psychiatry Reports* 16, no. 9 (September 27, 2014): 464. https://doi.org/10.1007/s11920-014-0464-x.

# Hire Blythe Landry
## To Speak and Coach

Inspire your team or your organization to move beyond the frequent divide between human emotion and workplace productivity. Offer the people whom you serve the opportunity to learn from a truly dynamic, engaged, and innovative speaker and trainer who cares about the needs of each individual, as well as the growth and expansion of your group as a whole.

Blythe is a seasoned speaker, trainer, and presenter who is successful at navigating and leading groups of myriad demographics and sizes, as well as astute at using humor, story-telling, and relatable content to meet the unique needs of each group dynamic.

Whether you are seeking to improve your leadership team's understanding and implementation of Trauma Intelligence, or you are seeking to address this at a special event or for a larger scale educational endeavor, Blythe will work with you to create a truly special and individualized program.

In addition to her expertise on trauma and Trauma Intelligence, Blythe is also an expert trainer and presenter on grief/loss, addiction(s), and team cohesion and communication(s).

Book your next training or event featuring Blythe Landry, LCSW, M.Ed. by visiting blythelandry.com.

 @blythelandrycoach

blythelandry.com

www.ingramcontent.com/pod-product-compliance
Lightning Source LLC
Chambersburg PA
CBHW072019110526
44592CB00012B/1371